Copyright © 2024
All rights reserved.
Reedy Press
PO Box 5131
St. Louis, MO 63139
reedypress.com

No part of this publication may be reproduced or transmitted in any form or by any means, electronic or mechanical, including photocopy, recording, or any information storage and retrieval system, without permission in writing from the publisher. Permissions may be sought directly from Reedy Press at the above mailing address or via our website at reedypress.com.

Library of Congress Control Number: 2024930394

ISBN: 9781681065021

Printed in the United States of America
24 25 26 27 28   5 4 3 2 1

Cover and title page art courtesy of Dan Zettwoch.
Images courtesy of Tara Smith unless marked.
Line art courtesy of FreePik, Shutterstock, or believed to be in the public domain.

We (the publisher and the author) have done our best to provide the most accurate information available when this book was completed. However, we make no warranty, guarantee, or promise about the accuracy, completeness, or currency of the information provided, and we expressly disclaim all warranties, express or implied. Please note that attractions, company names, addresses, websites, and phone numbers are subject to change or closure, and this is outside of our control. We are not responsible for any loss, damage, injury, or inconvenience that may occur due to the use of this book. When exploring new destinations, please do your homework before you go. You are responsible for your own safety and health when using this book.

Dedication

This book is first and foremost dedicated to my husband, Steven, and kids, Parker, Ivy, Graham, and Darcy. Without your help and support, none of this would have been possible. You are my everything. So many thanks also to my friends who have cheered me on along the way and to my parents for always believing in me and encouraging me from a young age to keep writing stories.

Table of Contents

Introduction 1
Best Place to Feel like a Tourist 2
Best Place for Something You've Never Done Before 4
Best Place to Take Someone Visiting from Out of Town.... 6
Best Playground 8
Best Place for Toddlers 10
Best Place for Elementary-Age Kids 12
Best Place for Teenagers 14
Best Place for Big Age Gaps 16
Best Place to Spend a Day Off School 18
Best Place to Go on a Rainy Day 20
Best Place with a Free Zip Line 22
Best Easy Hike 24
Best Place to Experience River Wild 26
Best Smaller Water Adventure 28
Best Place for Camping 30
Best Day Trip 32
Best Historical Place 34
Best Bike Trail 36
Best Place for the Animal Lover 38
Best Place for Educational Outdoors 40
Best Place to Go Fishing 42
Best Fun Run 44
Best Place for Geocaching 46
Best Place to Learn All about Lewis and Clark 48
Best Farmers Market 50
Best Pick-Your-Own Farm 52

Best Ways to Volunteer	54
Best Place to Read a Book	56
Best Place to Buy a Book	58
Best Library for Kids	60
Best Place to Get a Frozen Treat	62
Best Place for a Celebratory Treat	64
Best Theme Restaurant	66
Best Place to Take Picky Eaters	68
Best Place to Take an Out-of-Towner to Eat	70
Best Place for the Little Carnivore	72
Best Breakfast	74
Best Place to Learn to Get Cooking	76
Best Mini Golf	78
Best Place to Learn to Play Golf	80
Best Bowling Alley	82
Best Place to See Smaller Sports Teams	84
Best Outdoor Place for Family Pictures	86
Best Selfie and Instagram Photo Ops	88
Best Staycation	90
Best Place for Your Car Enthusiast	92
Best Place for the Train Enthusiast	94
Best Place to Take a Plane Enthusiast	96
Best Place for Kids Who Love Science	98
Best Ice-Skating Rinks	100
Best Place to Spin Your Wheels	102
Best Swimming Pool	104
Best Place for Thrill Seekers	106
Best Freebie	108
Best Place to Have a Birthday Party	110
Best At-Home Birthday Party Add-On	112

Best Place to See Santa 114
Best Holiday Lights... 116
Best Festival 118
Best Membership 120
Best Place to Introduce Kids to Live Theater....................... 122
Best Place to Introduce Art... 124
Best Place to Introduce Music 126
Best Splash Pad... 128
Best Ropes Course 130
Best Place for Fall Fun 132
Best Toy Store.. 134
Best Place to Buy Comics and Games 136
Best Sweet Treats 138
Best Arcade.. 140
Best Place to Go Sledding 142
Best Nursery for Family Gardening....................................... 144
Best Activity with the Family Dog 146
Best Movie Theater 148
Index 150

Introduction

I've been exploring St. Louis with my kids for over 15 years. And before that, I spent my own childhood discovering many of the fun places this awesome city has to offer.

St. Louis is filled with so many unique and interesting places that are perfect for families. In *Best Mom St. Louis* I've tried to collect the best St. Louis has to offer . . . and there's a lot! There are old favorites like Tower Tee, the Gateway Arch, or riding the carousel at Faust Park or the Saint Louis Zoo. But there are also great places to visit that you may not know about. Experience some epic indoor fun on a rainy day at Kids Empire in Ballwin, take a ride with Gateway Helicopter Tours, or go a little retro and introduce your kids to Popeye—the sailor, not the chicken—and walk the Popeye Trail in Chester, Illinois, home of cartoonist Elzie C. Segar.

Whether you're interested in hiking, the arts, entertainment, or any other activity, there are countless categories that will fit your family. I hope you'll be inspired to pile the kids in the car and get out and explore the city you already know and love, while being the best mom!

Best Place to Feel like a Tourist

RIVERBOAT TOUR

50 S Leonor K. Sullivan Blvd. | 877-982-1410
gatewayarch.com/experience/riverboat-cruises

You'll climb aboard a boat named *Tom Sawyer*, fitting for the theme of the Mississippi! The Riverboats at the Gateway Arch have a variety of different cruises on the Mississippi River to choose from. All ages will love cruising in front of the Arch by way of 19th-century replica paddle wheel boats. Plan a special night out with the kids by taking a dinner cruise and seeing the lights of downtown sparkling on the stainless steel of the Arch, or climb aboard the *Becky Thatcher* for a popular Sunday brunch. There's even a specially designed Riverboat Explorer Junior Ranger Program for kids to learn about the history of river travel and more, so there's no shortage of fun found here for kids and families to enjoy.

✓ How to be a best mom:

- Point out the *Captains' Return* statue as you go along the riverfront.
- When you go ashore, plan to get some eats at the waterfront dining location that is Paddlewheel Café.

Courtesy of Riverboats at the Gateway Arch

Enjoy some of the best views of the Gateway Arch!

ST. LOUIS GATEWAY ARCH

11 N 4th St. | 877-982-1410 | gatewayarch.com

You'll get the best view of the Old Courthouse! From the top of the stainless steel sparkler, you can look out rectangular-shaped windows to see the courthouse's outer rotunda from above. The treasure of the Lou, in the form of a 630-foot-tall metal arch, shines along the river by day and reflects the city lights by night. Since its opening in the fall of 1965, the Gateway to the West has been welcoming guests from around the world. The museum below the Arch, as well as the grounds outside, are free and open to the public. There is a fee to go to the top of the Arch and to watch a film about the construction, but both are worth the cost of admission. Interactive exhibits and artifacts fill the museum space, making this a great educational trip for any local tourist.

- Take a stroll around the Arch grounds and walk down the steps that are in front of the river.
- Check in at the information desk to sign kids up for the Junior Ranger Program.

SAINT LOUIS TROLLEY

999 N 2nd St. | 314-241-1400 | stltrolley.com

You'll feel nostalgic for the way St. Louisans used to travel! While the days of the streetcar are long gone in downtown, families can still take a tour in a trolley car. These trolleys are outfitted with climate control, comfortable seats, and large windows to look out at the city's skyscrapers so it's not exact to what residents experienced in days gone by. A bright red trolley that matches our beloved Cardinals' color will take you along the Mississippi River, by the Cathedral Basilica of St. Louis, or into Forest Park. Kids will be in awe of Millionaire's Row and enjoy the educational tidbits of the tour. There are various tours to choose from, and you can even take the trolley to see holiday lights at Our Lady of the Snows or Candy Cane Lane. It's a fun trip for the entire family to enjoy seeing downtown from a totally different perspective.

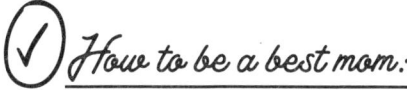

- Take a ride on a historic trolley at the Museum of Transportation.
- Continue the going-back-in-time feel by planning a time to visit Dad's Cookie Company at 3854 Louisiana Ave.

Best Place for Something You've Never Done Before

BUSCH STADIUM TOURS

700 Clark St. | 314-345-9000
mlb.com/cardinals/ballpark/tours

You'll see your favorite baseball stadium like never before! Tours of Busch Stadium have been taking place since its opening in 2006 and are quite popular among locals and visitors. But have you ever done a tour before as a family? Instead of heading to the seating areas or getting a snack at concessions, like you would during a game, the tour guide will lead you through the concourses to see private club areas and the broadcast booth. Learn all about team history by choosing one of two tours: the Classic Tour includes admission to the legendary Cardinals Hall of Fame and Museum, or get the best views of the stadium on the 360 Tour. No matter the weather or time of year, tours are taking place so it's the perfect family activity for whenever you want to be taken out to the ball game.

✓ How to be a best mom:

- Stop by the Official Cardinals Team Store to get some Cardinals-themed merchandise.
- Grab some ice cream from the Prairie Farms vending machine outside in Ballpark Village.

GATEWAY HELICOPTER TOURS

50 N Leonor K. Sullivan Blvd. | 314-496-4494
gatewayhelicoptertours.com

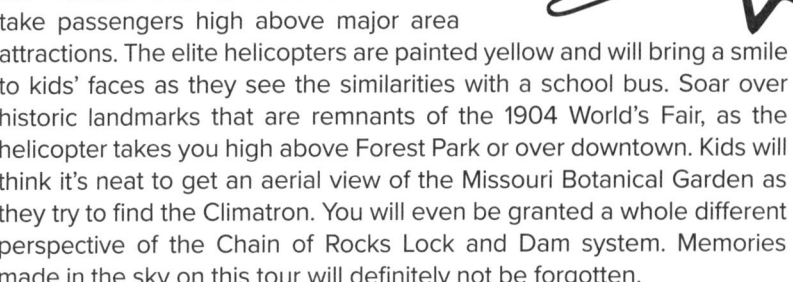

You'll be not just on top of the world but on top of St. Louis! This helicopter adventure has various tours to choose from that take passengers high above major area attractions. The elite helicopters are painted yellow and will bring a smile to kids' faces as they see the similarities with a school bus. Soar over historic landmarks that are remnants of the 1904 World's Fair, as the helicopter takes you high above Forest Park or over downtown. Kids will think it's neat to get an aerial view of the Missouri Botanical Garden as they try to find the Climatron. You will even be granted a whole different perspective of the Chain of Rocks Lock and Dam system. Memories made in the sky on this tour will definitely not be forgotten.

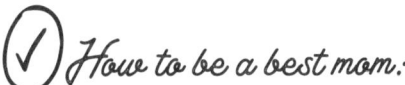

- If you have an addition coming to the family, older siblings will get a kick out of a gender reveal color being sprayed from the helicopter.
- Take a look at the historic Eads Bridge on the riverfront.

THIRD DEGREE GLASS FACTORY

5200 Delmar Blvd. | 314-367-4527
thirddegreeglassfactory.com

You'll learn how blown glass is made up close and personal! Anyone age 10 and older can sign up for a private glassblowing session. Everything you need to create your own unique piece is included, and this makes a great experience gift. Pick the colors you want to use and style to be made, and then work directly with a skilled glass artist to create something that you will cherish for years to come. There are also all sorts of ready-made colorful glass vases, bowls, paperweights, jewelry, and decorative tiles that can be found for purchase in the on-site shop. It's unlike anything you've ever experienced and something the older kids will enjoy doing.

- Get a blown glass Christmas tree ornament (or other type of holiday decoration) to enjoy year after year.
- Attend a Third Friday event for a unique and fun family activity.

Best Place to Take Someone Visiting from Out of Town

CITY MUSEUM

750 N 16th St. | 314-231-2489
citymuseum.org

You'll think you entered a different world! Out-of-towners are often told to visit this unique museum and for good reason, because there's nothing else quite like it. The entire museum is a world of wonder to explore with tunnels that go underfoot and slides that are several stories tall. Younger kids can easily get lost in the many man-made caves so you will want to stay together. For an additional fee, guests who enjoy heights will think the rooftop is well worth it. Atop the roof you'll find giant slides, climbing structures, and a Ferris wheel, all 10 stories above the ground. In the main part of the museum, there's even a specially designed toddler area, making this truly the place for the entire family to enjoy.

✓ How to be a best mom:

- Get a membership so you can go back again and again all year long. It's a great way to save, and select memberships will allow you to bring a friend as well as get discounts on food and retail.
- Add some fun onto the admission in the form of access to the Pinball Hall or take a guided tour.

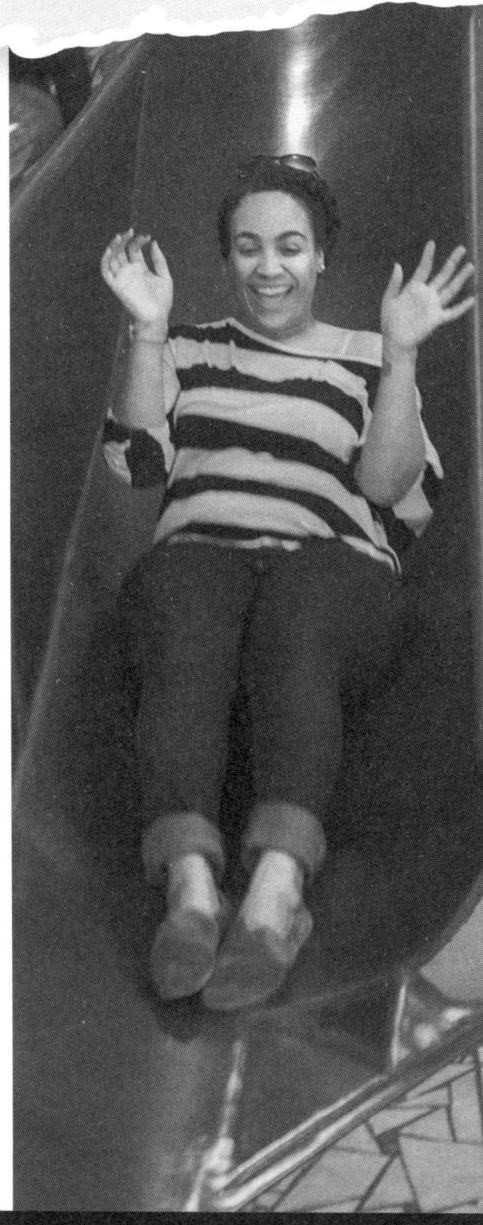

Courtesy of Don Korte

SAINT LOUIS ZOO

1 Government Dr. | 314-781-0900 | stlzoo.org

You'll be shocked by the cost of this zoo! While the zoo itself is free, there are so many fun paid attractions that are worth experiencing, like the sea lion show, touching stingrays, and the ever-popular train ride. Consistently voted one of the best zoos in the United States, this is the place to wow your visiting family and friends. At 90 acres, this zoo covers a significant amount of Forest Park. The setting itself is parklike with tall trees throughout to match the surrounding aesthetic. Kids will especially like being splashed by penguins as they swim by in their chilly exhibit and seeing a polar bear moving around his habitat. There's so much for the entire family that I'm not able to describe it all here.

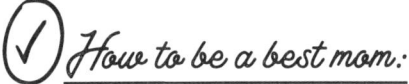

- Get tickets to take a ride on the Conservation Carousel.
- Book a behind-the-scenes tour to interact up close with a penguin or feed a tortoise.

CATHEDRAL BASILICA OF ST. LOUIS

4431 Lindell Blvd. | 314-373-8200
cathedralstl.org

You'll think you are in Italy! Known as "the Rome of the West," this cathedral is both stunning and historic. Filled with intricate mosaics and one-of-a-kind art, it's a place that your guests will only experience in St. Louis. While it is an active place of worship, tours are given and encouraged as opposed to the self-guided option, because you never know when the basilica will be in use for a wedding or church service. The sheer size of this domed cathedral will have kids in awe. Whether you're religious or not, it's a part of St. Louis history that is a great activity for the entire family.

- Take along a sketchbook with colored pencils, pick out a section of mosaic tiles, and have kids draw what they see.
- Attend a concert at the basilica.

Best Playground

SHAW PARK

27 S Brentwood Blvd., Clayton | 314-290-8500
claytonmo.gov/Home/Components/FacilityDirectory/FacilityDirectory/16/314

You'll be able to explore in a tree house without ever climbing a ladder! Situated between the northern parking lot and North Shelter, the Treetop Playground is all about inclusivity and accessibility. The entire playground lies inside a gated fence, creating an extra safety feature for keeping tabs on kids as they run and play. Various ramps lead up to the equipment landings, including to that of the tree house. Kids will have a blast going down standard slides, ones that twist, and even a roller slide. There are several types of swings, a uniquely designed teeter-totter, and a splash pad for the summer months. An ample amount of picnic tables, perfect for a lunch or snack, are next to the playground. This park is a fun location for all ages.

✓ How to be a best mom:

- Take a stroll through the Sensory Garden located just beyond the fence situated behind the tree house.
- Be sure to explore the architecturally and aesthetically modern playground with climbing ropes that is farther in the park by the ball fields.

SENSORY GARDEN

INDIAN CAMP CREEK PARK

2679 Dietrich Rd., Foristell | 636-949-7535
sccmo.org/665/Indian-Camp-Creek-Park

You'll want to travel to this park again and again! It's a bit of a drive out of town but well worth taking the adventure. Resting just beyond the banks of a large, stocked lake for fishing, this playground has everything that kids can possibly dream up. Slides, swings, and rock structures to climb can be seen everywhere you turn. There are various types of climbing nets scattered throughout, including one on the massive fortlike climbing structure. Kids will love exploring the net-enclosed catwalks that are up high connecting the parts of the fort, and there's even a merry-go-round that is enclosed by rope netting. When it comes to cooling off, there's a small splash pad with man-made canals to wade in and a large, shaded pavilion for beating the heat.

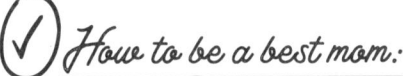

How to be a best mom:

- Play Frisbee golf.
- Hire a photographer to take the popular family photos of you splashing and wading through the natural creek that runs on the park property.

BRENTWOOD PARK

2924 Brazeau Ave., Brentwood | 314-963-8689
brentwoodmo.org/2437/Brentwood-Park

You're destined to have fun! It's not often that a true destination playground comes along, and this one is for the ages. So much thought went into these 2.7 acres of fun. The community was asked what they would like to see in a playground, and those ideas were brought to fruition, particularly with the zip line that's 100 feet long. Kids will love the Viking Swing, Orchid Climber, and Adventure Fort. There are separate play areas for older kids and younger kids, with specially designed inclusive features so all children can enjoy this state-of-the-art playground. Other standouts are the 30-foot slide that descends from a hill and a splash pad with waterfall. Enough cannot be said about this incredible playground.

How to be a best mom:

- Take along your bikes as this park connects to the Great Rivers Greenway system.
- Plan a time to go ice-skating at the local Brentwood Community Center.

Best Place for Toddlers

PLAY STREET MUSEUM

1650 Beale St., Ste. 138, St. Charles | 314-471-0065
stlouis.playstreetmuseum.com

You'll step right into unique playhouses! Absolutely darling and filled with imagination, this child-size village is immediately captivating. The indoor play area consists of intricately detailed buildings that have shorter doorways perfect for toddlers to feel right at home. Once a taller person bends down to step through, however, each individual building opens up on the inside from floor to ceiling, making it possible for a grown adult to fully stand. The space is alive with color and includes a pretend grocery store, house, café, pet rescue, doctor's office, and firehouse complete with a slide and fire truck.

Perfect for toddlers to feel right at home!

✓ How to be a best mom:

- Is your child getting overwhelmed? Look for the Discovery Rug or building bricks area; both are set away from the action.
- Add creating a craft or custom slime to the admission.

GRANDMA'S PLAYROOM

9981 Lin Ferry Dr. | 314-270-3291 | grandmasplayroomstl.com

You'll be part of a community! This play space is popular with the locals, but it also has visitors from all over. It's a great place to meet other toddler moms or to gather with friends. The owner, Sierra Zagarri, is a well-known YouTuber and it's apparent that she brings her eye for creativity into this business as well. All around the playroom you will find colorful murals on the walls that help to section off the different themed areas, and there's even a separate fenced-in infant area for kids 24 months and younger. Kids will love exploring the different stations around the room, especially the playroom's pride and joy, a large wooden climbing tower. Train fans will love playing at the massive train table with the middle cut out that allows access to the center.

✓ How to be a best mom:

- Attend a special event at the playroom like story time, a craft activity, or Saturday morning yoga.
- Book a private family night at the playroom.

MAJOR LEE BERRA CREATION STATION

2933 Barrett Station Rd. | 314-965-6212 | tnmot.org

You'll be tempted to sing "Little Red Caboose" the minute you step in the door! The floor-to-ceiling murals painted in colorful scenes are dedicated to trains chugging across the countryside and cars driving through town. Even the floor underfoot is colorful and fun in this inviting space. Perfect for ages less than 5 years, this play space inside the National Museum of Transportation is all about things that go. Named in honor of a United States Air Force pilot who died in an airplane crash, this playroom has tables for trains and building blocks. Kids will enjoy playing together or independently. Climbing aboard a school bus that's just their size or being imaginative in the wooden kitchen set is sure to be a favorite activity. Kids can even pretend to mail a letter. Your little toddler will want to spend time with you here again and again or have their birthday in this fun space.

✓ How to be a best mom:

- Get tickets to the handcar or mini train ride just outside.
- Find a unique gift in the Boxcar Boutique.

Best Place for Elementary-Age Kids

THE MAGIC HOUSE MADE FOR KIDS

5127 Delmar Blvd. | 314-328-0561 | magichouse.org/MADE

You'll climb to a second-floor makerspace that's designed just for kids! The setting has a city loft feel and is well thought out with a designated area for just about every craft you can think of. Its name MADE actually stands for Makers, Artists, Designers & Entrepreneurs, and that's just what kids will find around every turn. Learning how to sew, building creations with recycled materials, watching a demonstration of the pottery wheel, and making a custom button are just a few of the fun opportunities. No one says you can't bring in your own beads to string at the crafting tables or preferred paints from home, but kids are free to use the supplies in the space. Kids who like technology will particularly be drawn to the areas for 3D printing, laser cutting, and stop-motion filmmaking. Every so often there's a new traveling exhibit in the center of the space so go back to explore again and again.

✓ *How to be a best mom:*

- Arrange to have your kids' clay creations fired and glazed in the kiln.
- Sign up for private lessons to learn screen printing or how to use the pottery wheel.

A designated area for just about every craft you can think of!

MYSEUM

283 Lamp and Lantern Village, Town and Country
636-220-7930 | stlmyseum.com

You'll have a science-filled fun time! Exhibits abound throughout this expansive children's museum. Much of the inside's perimeter is dedicated to science with stations featuring things like an air vortex cannon, infrared thermal detection, electricity, sound, and so much more. Kids will talk nonstop about finding the swamp monster in the maze that's built with hundreds of hanging pool noodles that must be pushed through. The radar slide is also a highlight because it tracks just how fast kids slide down. There's a giant inflatable spaceship in the center of the museum, a fantastic bounce house, and a spectacular light show that plays every hour on the hour at the Tesla Coil. This is the perfect place for a day off school, a rainy day, or a celebration.

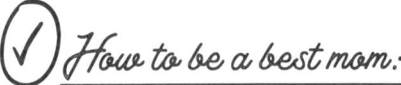
How to be a best mom:

- Don't miss the zoo vet center that's tucked away in the back corner.
- Set up your camera in the shadow room to take video of the shadows kids make on the wall.

PURINA FARMS

500 William Danforth Way, Gray Summit | 888-688-7387
purina.com/about-purina/purina-farms

You'll spend time with animal friends! From a petting arena to cow milking to an incredible dog show, kids will have fun learning all about the animals at this free farm. Don't miss the stairs that wrap up and around to a truly unique cat house; this structure was built to a massive size of 20 feet tall and features multiple levels that the farm's feline friends can roam in. While this farm is typically only open to the public from April to October, there are special events throughout the year, especially for the holidays. Kids will particularly love visiting for the not-so-scary Howl-o-ween Fest and the festively decorated Pet-acular Holiday Bazaar.

How to be a best mom:

- If you've been wanting to add a furry member of the family, ask about the dogs and cats that are up for adoption in the pet center.
- Request that a virtual birthday greeting be sent to your child from the Purina Farms animals.

Best Place for Teenagers

WORLD CHESS HALL OF FAME

4652 Maryland Ave., Ste. 1
314-367-9243 | worldchesshof.org

You'll visit the world's largest chess piece! The giant King of the Central West End is 20 feet tall, weighs over 10,800 pounds, and sits outside of this impressive hall of fame. Chess champions have been made here. Teens will enjoy any number of the programs offered just for them by the St. Louis Chess Club that is also housed at the WCHOF. There are even private lessons available for all levels. With family activities and exhibits taking place throughout the year, it's a great place for everyone to enjoy, but particularly the perfect place for teens to learn some of the more complex chess moves. Or there are introductory learn-to-play classes for teenagers who are just starting out.

✓ How to be a best mom:

- Purchase your chess player a special gift of a carved wood chess set from the Q Bout!que.
- Grab some breakfast or lunch at the chess-themed diner, Kingside, across the street.

UPPER LIMITS ROCK GYM & PRO SHOP

1874 Lackland Hill Pkwy., Maryland Heights | 314-991-2516
upperlimits.com

You'll climb mountains in the Midwest! A great activity for conquering new heights and learning new skills, this rock-climbing facility has boulders and walls to scale up. While there are several locations to choose from, the Maryland Heights gym is perfectly located for most areas. It's easy to grasp onto the colorful hand holds at the same time as you push upward with your feet, all while harnessed in with a secure rope. Teens will have fun with this activity and gain self-confidence no matter how high they climb, because they tried something new.

- Save with a student ID on Wednesday nights or on family/youth night on Fridays.
- Suggest to your school's PTO or church organization to have a portable rock wall at an event.

DISC GOLF

With countless disc golf courses in the St. Louis area, you don't have to travel far to find a location near you. This sport is great for most everyone in the family to enjoy, but particularly for teens to get outside and learn a new skill. From Jefferson Barracks Park in South County to Carrollton Park in Bridgeton, there are all levels of courses to choose from. There's a picturesque course in the park across from Creve Coeur Lake, and Logan University even has a course right on campus for the entire community to enjoy. Most of the courses have the standard 18 holes, but there are a few with only nine. To get started, simply purchase a disc or two from your local sporting goods store and head to a park near you.

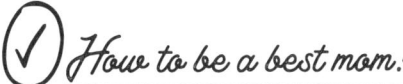

- Encourage your teen to join a local league to learn more about the sport and to perfect their skills.
- Teach your kids how to play the similar sport of ultimate Frisbee.

Best Place for Big Age Gaps

THE ST. LOUIS WHEEL

201 S 18th St. | 314-923-3960 | thestlouiswheel.com

You'll get a bird's-eye view of the St. Louis skyline that you won't see from anywhere else! This 200-foot-tall attraction is perfect for the entire family (up to eight in one gondola) to enjoy together. The view will be different by day or night so be sure to take that into consideration. At night the wheel is lit up to be seen from afar so most kids will find that to be quite magical. If a fear of heights is a concern, don't reserve the VIP gondola with its glass floor. Book this even more specially designed gondola if you want to up the thrill factor and are up for a unique experience. All gondolas are climate controlled, making this attraction doable 365 days a year.

Up the thrill factor with a glass-floor gondola!

✓ *How to be a best mom:*

- Get combo tickets to also ride the St. Louis Union Station Carousel and play mini golf.
- Walk down the boardwalk to see the koi fish in the Union Station lake.

CIRCUS FLORA

3401 Washington Ave. | 314-827-3830
circusflora.org

You'll experience a circus unlike any other! The big top found in the Grand Center District has a rich history and as a nonprofit organization does more than just entertain the community. For over 30 years this show has been wowing audiences with gravity-defying tightrope acts, high-flying aerial skills, juggling artists, talented animals, comedic clowns, and so much more. Each year there's a new and totally different story to be told through the circus acts. Kids of all ages will love watching the mystery unfold. There's not a bad seat in the house, and you will be amazed by how close you are to the daring performances. This one-ring circus is an extravaganza for the entire family and an activity that you will want to repeat year after year.

✓ *How to be a best mom:*

- Purchase VIP tickets to have access to the hospitality tent for snacks and to meet some of the show's cast.
- Take a camel ride at intermission.

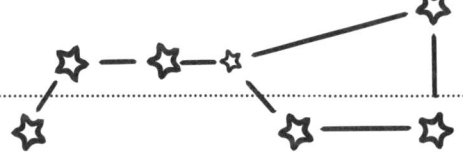

JAMES S. MCDONNELL PLANETARIUM

Clayton Ave. and Faulkner Dr. | 314-289-4400
slsc.org

You'll experience the wonders of space right in Forest Park! The retro outer concrete shell of McDonnell Planetarium at the Saint Louis Science Center itself looks like something that would launch off to outer space. First opened in 1959, today it's fitted with a ZEISS star projector that teaches people of all ages about the mysteries of space. Explore Mars with a remote-controlled rover and see what it was like to travel to the moon in a space capsule. Kids will also get a kick out of finding how much they would weigh on another planet. It's one of those traditions in St. Louis that families love to visit together all year long.

✓ *How to be a best mom:*

- Make sure to check out the F-18 Blue Angel outside of the planetarium, and you also might run into some dinosaurs.
- Teens and older kids will enjoy the special evening events like the laser light shows.

Best Place to Spend a Day Off School

ULYSSES S. GRANT NATIONAL HISTORIC SITE

7400 Grant Rd. | 314-842-1867 | nps.gov/ulsg

You'll take steps where a president of the United States once walked and lived! The grounds are serene and shaded by enormous oak trees. You can take a tour of White Haven, the historic residence that's painted in Paris Green, and watch a movie about the site in the museum's theater. Kids will enjoy taking pictures in the wooden cutouts of Ulysses S. Grant and Julia Dent and dressing up in period reproduction clothing that's inside the restored horse stable. At the stable exit there's a wagon and antique farm equipment that are interesting to see.

The Junior Ranger Program, booklets about which can be picked up at the information desk, is fun for kids to both participate in and feel accomplishment upon completion of.

✓ How to be a best mom:

- Take a walk on Grant's Trail to see the Clydesdales grazing behind the white fences along the trail.
- Don't miss the Little Free Library out front to take or donate a book.

ST. LOUIS CAROUSEL

15055 Faust Pk. Dr., Chesterfield | 314-615-8345
stlouiscarousel.com

You'll take a ride on part of St. Louis history! This unique carousel survived the fire at Forest Park Highlands (a popular theme park that was destroyed in 1963) and went on to be an attraction that was kept outside at Sylvan Springs Park. To better preserve the carousel's intricately painted horses, deer, and sleighs, it was moved to its current indoor and climate-controlled space in the late 1980s. Memberships are available to enjoy the carousel again and again. Kids will be delighted with the musical sounds and lights as they take a spin around on their seat of choice.

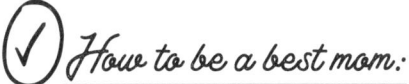

How to be a best mom:

- Be on the lookout for special events throughout the year.
- Take a picnic lunch to enjoy at Faust Park, which is on the same grounds.

ANNE O'C. ALBRECHT NATURE PLAYSCAPE

Along Concourse Dr.
forestparkforever.org/playscape

You'll explore a playground made from nature! While this isn't the typical playground with slides and swings, it's one that is sure to become a favorite destination. Right in the heart of Forest Park, this 17-acre stretch of land that falls in between the Jewel Box and World's Fair Pavilion was reconstituted into an area for play that opened in 2021. The natural playground "equipment" is composed of hollowed-out logs, waterfalls that flow into a small pond, tree stumps of varying heights, boulders to climb on, and so many pathways to run along playing hide-and-seek. Kids will enjoy walking along the Sensory Garden area to look for all the butterflies that are attracted to the flowers there.

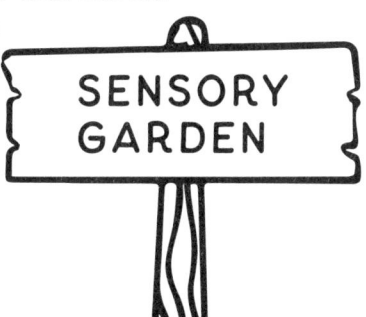

How to be a best mom:

- Have a change of shoes (and possibly clothes) on hand in the car in case kids get muddy or wet from the water features.
- Take a picnic to enjoy in the area or eat on the steps of the nearby World's Fair Pavilion.

Best Place to Go on a Rainy Day

SOPHIA M. SACHS BUTTERFLY HOUSE

15050 Faust Pk. Dr., Chesterfield | 314-577-0888
missouribotanicalgarden.org/plan-your-visit/family-of-attractions/butterfly-house

You'll love when a butterfly lands on your shoulder! Or you'll scream in terror. It really depends on your individual comfort level. The uniquely constructed Conservatory Garden opened in 1998, and while it's not a typical petting zoo, most kids will be delighted by the close contact with butterflies. The constant year-round temperature of 82 degrees makes this tropical ecosystem an especially welcome escape on a rainy day or during the winter months. There are fun events throughout the year, lots of educational opportunities, and a gift shop filled with unique gift ideas.

✓ How to be a best mom:

- Plan to experience (usually in February or March) when more than 1,000 blue morpho butterflies fill the conservatory.
- Go back on a sunny day to walk the outdoor pathways and enjoy the butterfly garden.

Courtesy of Don Korte

POWDER VALLEY CONSERVATION NATURE CENTER

11715 Cragwold Rd., Kirkwood | 314-301-1500
mdc.mo.gov/discover-nature/places/powder-valley-conservation-nature-center

You'll experience the outdoors indoors! While the outdoor portion of this 112-acre property features the natural habitat of Mother Earth, visitors will find so much to do when the weather sends them indoors. This nature center has an indoor play tree house, aquariums, an active beehive (viewable from in between glass), and two floors of educational areas. Kids can see what it's like to look through the distorted vision of a fly and will learn about conservation in a whole new way. Even making leaf rubbings with crayons, paper, and metal-cast nature shapes is an option for indoor fun. Don't be surprised if you are tempted to head outside in the rain, as the hiking trails will call to you—or be sure to go back on a nice day to explore the entire area.

✓  How to be a best mom:

- Look ahead for upcoming events that are taking place. There are educational experiences and musical performances for various ages.
- Watch your kids perform a puppet show.

KIDS EMPIRE

14882 Manchester Rd., Ballwin | 636-200-3961 | ballwin.kidsempire.com

You'll play on an epic playground that's indoors! Not just a kingdom for kids, this is an entire empire. The space has everything imaginable. From straight slides of various sizes to ones with rolling hills, kids will love racing each other down. There are maze obstacle courses to explore in the massive climbing towers that connect via net bridges and balance beams. A miniature soccer arena has just the right amount of room for kicking the ball around, and you will want to get out on the dance floor to show your kids all the moves from your younger years. Going beyond a traditional playground, there's a motorbike track, ride-ons, trikes, and a separate toddler area. This is definitely the place to go when kids are begging to play at the park on a rainy day.

✓  How to be a best mom:

- Get a punch card to both save on admission and be all set to return again and again.
- Book a birthday party that is sure to be the talk of the friends circle.

21

Best Place with a Free Zip Line

RAYBURN PARK

746 Rayburn Ave. | 314-729-4700
cityofcrestwood.org/facilities/facility/details/rayburnpark-3

You'll feel like you're on a roller coaster! This zip line is definitely for the older and braver kids, because it's quite intense. A standard playground swing is attached to a rail that goes out and around for at least 60 feet. Daredevils take a pretty significant drop from a ramp and then cruise around swinging back and forth. The ride ends at a separate ramp on the side of the playground structure. Kids will find this extreme zip line to be thrilling and a memorable time. The park itself is on over three acres and the playground sits atop a hill.

✓ How to be a best mom:

- Take a cooler with some Popsicles to enjoy under one of the shade trees that surround the playground.
- Bring your bikes to hit nearby Grant's Trail.

Kids will find this extreme zip line thrilling and memorable!

VAGO PARK

2700 Fee Fee Rd., Maryland Heights | 314-738-2599
marylandheights.com/departments/parks_and_recreation/city_parks___trails.php

You'll soar through the air at the same time as someone else! This park has two types of zip lines that run parallel to each other. More adventurous kids will take a leap onto a rope swing with disc seat. There's also an ADA-accessible seat that glides on the track. This revolutionary seat allows for access by more children with its lock-in-place harness. Smaller kids will enjoy this type of seat as well. Kids will enjoy racing each other on this fun double zip line. The playground as a whole is really spectacular.

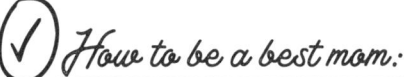

- Burn some calories of your own on the fitness course that is adjacent to the playground.
- Take your kids to the amazing splash pad (complete with a bucket dump and rainbow rings) found near the entrance of the park.

WATSON TRAIL PARK

12450 W Watson Rd. | 314-842-7265
sunset-hills.com/453/Watson-Trail-Park

You'll find a zip line that is hidden among nature! While the main playground at the entrance of this park is state of the art and quite popular with varying equipment for all ages, the zip line is where kids like to congregate. Take a short walk down a paved hill and go past the pond to find a second playground that's a fun favorite. The entire area is filled with tall shade trees, and the zip line is the perfect size for big and little kids. It's not the longest ride but rather a rope swing type with a circular seat that is manageable for kids of various ages. This great park is sure to become a family favorite again and again due mainly to its fun-filled atmosphere.

- Play disc golf.
- Take quarters to use in the machines to purchase corn for feeding the ducks.

Best Easy Hike

MERAMEC GREENWAY AND WESTERN GREENWAY

Hwy. 109 and Old State Rd., Wildwood (historic Glencoe)
greatriversgreenway.org

You'll go on two easy hikes in one location! On the Meramec Greenway kids will marvel at the size of the tall limestone bluffs that line much of the path and enjoy hearing sounds of the river flowing just beyond the trees. Walk along just a half mile to the overlook. Animals like whitetail deer, red fox, rabbits, turtles, frogs, and raccoons make their home along the Meramec River areas so keep your eyes peeled. Underfoot is completely level, packed small gravel. Running in the opposite direction is the Western Greenway, completely paved and also an easy trail that is just 1.5 miles in length. Both of these trails are a must for a family looking for a stroll outdoors.

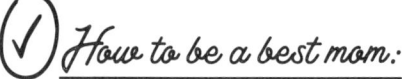

- Play nature hunt bingo as you meander along the trail.
- Plan some extra time for the nearby playground.

MYRON AND SONYA GLASSBERG FAMILY CONSERVATION AREA

Route FF S, Eureka | 636-441-4554
mdc.mo.gov/discover-nature/places/myron-sonya-glassberg-family-conservation-area

You'll think you are hiking multiple locations at one time! Just a short distance away in Eureka is 429 acres of protected land that has so many different things to see. The terrain of this unique conservation area varies from rocky areas with small inclines and hills to grassy open spaces, but overall, the under-three-mile loop is an easy one. Kids will love exploring and climbing on the large rock formations. There are a few small waterfalls and streams to enjoy. Along the trail are some monuments with quotes to inspire, like the Native American proverb, "We do not inherit the earth from our ancestors; we borrow it from our children." This hike is definitely worth the drive and is one that you will want to go back to.

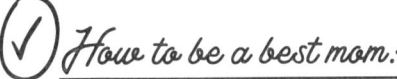

How to be a best mom:

- Treat looking for a popular Henry David Thoreau quote as a treasure hunt. (It's on a red metal plaque attached to a large rock along the trail.)
- Go in the springtime when the water features will be flowing at their peak.

QUEENY PARK

550 Weidman Rd. | 1675 S Mason Rd.
stlouiscountymo.gov/st-louis-county-departments/parks/places/queeny-park

You'll find more than one easy hike! For over 40 years the main attraction of this park has quite arguably been its iconic playscape, but there's so much more to explore in this 564-acre park. With more than five trails shorter than one mile in length, this is the place for everyone in the family to enjoy a hike together. Even some of the longer hikes aren't that strenuous—that is if you don't finish them in their entirety. Areas just off the trail will range from wooded shade to open green spaces. The Dogwood Trail gets its name from the beautiful trees that bloom bright white in spring, making it a hike you for sure do not want to miss out on seasonally. Going back again and again means there's another easy hike to enjoy the next time.

How to be a best mom:

- All kids will enjoy the new inclusive playground that is replacing the 1970s structures, so be sure to visit when it opens.
- Get a day pass to take your four-legged member of the family to the Tails and Trails Dog Park.

Best Place to Experience River Wild

MERAMEC RIVER

1135 Hwy. W, Sullivan | 573-468-2283
americascave.com/river

Courtesy of Missouri State Parks

You'll have a floating good time! Float trips are a popular activity for many in the summer months as a relaxing way to cool off. Whether it's floating the river in a canoe, kayak, or raft, everyone's favorite caving company, Meramec Caverns, will outfit you with everything you need to adventure on the Meramec River. For the most part your watercraft will just float along with the current downstream, but you will have some oars to help with steering. A shuttle bus will take you upriver to start the float and then the trip will end back at your vehicle parked at Meramec Caverns. Along the way you will see rocky bluffs towering above and sandbars poking out of the water. There are even riverboat rides you can book on canopy-topped boats for a tour of this region of the Meramec River with even less work for you.

✓
How to be a best mom:

- Take a trip underground with a cave tour at Meramec Caverns.
- Go camping at local Meramec State Park.

Book a riverboat ride on a canopy-topped boat.

MISSISSIPPI RIVER

4662 Washington Blvd. | 314-896-4262
2muddy.com

You'll see downtown in an entirely different way while paddling down the mighty Mississippi! While St. Louis is built on the banks of the second-longest river in the country, most of its residents have only ever driven over it. Taking a specially built canoe down the muddy river is a wild adventure that allows families to feel much like the first settlers who came to the area. Big Muddy Adventures has expert guides to help you navigate downstream until you arrive at the Arch. There are a few trips to choose from, with some being longer and others micro adventures of less than an hour. You will pass under multiple bridges, all while taking in the St. Louis skyline from the water. If you are lucky, you will see a barge or steamboat making its way along the river. The trip is for kids 6 years and older and one that everyone will not soon forget.

✓ *How to be a best mom:*

- Sign up early, as these trips book up fast.
- Each child must have an adult chaperone, so plan accordingly.

HUZZAH RIVER

970 E Hwy. 8, Steelville | 800-367-4516
huzzahvalley.com

You'll adventure through some rapids! This river is popular for float trips due to the range of natural beauty you will see along the way and the parts where the water flows quickly. There are towering trees and bluffs that make for a peaceful setting in nature. The water is clear, and in some of the shallow areas you will have the opportunity to see pebbles covering the riverbed. As you meander downriver you will come across areas that are more quick flowing, creating rapids over rock ledges and downed trees. There are quite a few outfitters to set you up with everything you need for this float, but Huzzah Valley Resort has all you need for canoeing, kayaking, rafting, and even tubing down the river.

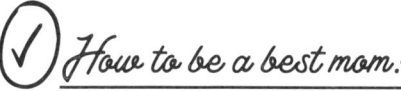

✓ *How to be a best mom:*

- Stay in a cabin at the Huzzah Valley Resort.
- Get a group of other families together to go floating with you.

Best Smaller Water Adventure

SIMPSON LAKE

1234 Marshall Rd., Valley Park | 314-710-8549 | paddlesimpsonlake.com

The entire family will want to set time aside for a lake excursion in Valley Park! Simpson Park is well known for its soccer fields, but also its majestic lake in the back part of the property. This 72-acre lake is man-made and is not typically overly busy. With the low-key and laid-back atmosphere, it's the perfect spot for beginners to be introduced to the sport of kayaking or paddleboarding. If you don't have your own watercraft to launch, there are one-hour rentals on a first-come, first-served basis right on-site. There are also canoe rentals if that type of boat is more your speed. Everyone in the family will think they are deep in the country, but occasionally the sounds of Interstate 44 will remind them that they are still in the city.

✓ How to be a best mom:

- Each child under 11 years of age must be in the same boat with a dedicated adult (to every one child), so plan accordingly to make sure you have enough adults.
- Cross the parking lot to explore the walking/biking trails and playground space.

CREVE COEUR LAKE

13171 Dripping Springs Rd., Maryland Heights | 314-330-4692
crevecoeurlakerentals.net

You'll want to do more than just boating! This large park in the middle of Creve Coeur is a destination not to miss out on. With its 320-acre lake, it's a great place to get out on the water. Kayaks, paddleboards, and canoes are all available to rent most of the year on a first-come, first-served basis. If you take out a canoe during the week, the rental is rent one hour and get an extra hour free, so take note of that way to save. As always you are welcome to bring your own small watercraft to launch. Kids will enjoy looking out to see if they can spot crew teams practicing or a sailboat cutting quickly across the water with the wind. There's Lakehouse Bar & Grill (on nearby Mallard Lake) with a refreshing root beer float or delectable sundae, so plan to stop in after being out on the water.

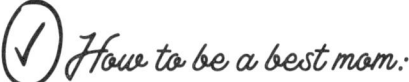

- Rent a surrey (two-person, four-wheeled bike) and go for a ride on the bike trail along the lake.
- Take a walk or bike down to the Dripping Springs Waterfall on the southeast side of the lake.

FOREST PARK BOATHOUSE

6101 Government Dr. | 314-798-2961 | paddleforestpark.com

You'll boat in the middle of everyone's favorite park! Whether it's choosing to see the museum sitting atop Art Hill by kayak, paddleboard, or canoe, all options are available to navigate over to the Emerson Grand Basin. There are even the popular paddleboats to be taken out on the water. Kids will want to pick out the color of paddleboat that will hold up to four passengers (can seat five with small children). From the docks of the boathouse, the entire family will love making memories while exploring Forest Park by water.

- Take a blanket along in your car and get some eats to go from the boathouse for a picnic across the suspension bridge on Picnic Island.
- Rent a bike to cruise around the many bike trails in Forest Park.

Best Place for Camping

KLONDIKE PARK

4600 S Missouri 94, Augusta
636-949-7535
sccmo.org/690/Klondike-Park

You'll experience white sand without traveling to the gulf! This St. Charles County place to camp is worth the drive. Both tent camping and cabin camping are available here. The cabins are primitive so no kitchens, but kids will think it's fun to sleep in the bunk beds. This park's natural landscape will make you feel like you've landed on another planet. Originally a quarry for mining silica, the resource is what has created the oddity that is a white sand beach in the Midwest. Parts of the park even give off a Yellowstone vibe with the rocky bluffs and vegetation. Kids will love building sandcastles on the beach, and there's a hike (both paved and more complex) for every level to enjoy.

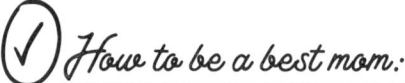

How to be a best mom:

- Swimming in the lake is not allowed, but your kids will love adventuring in/on rentable kayaks and stand-up paddleboards.

- Take along some beach toys so your kids can play in the sand.

BABLER STATE PARK

800 Guy Park Dr., Wildwood | 636-458-3813
mostateparks.com/park/dr-edmund-babler-memorial-state-park

You'll sleep under the stars if you don't take a tent! Founded as a tribute to Dr. Edmund Babler by his brother Jacob, this land donated to the state of Missouri started out at approximately 800 acres. Over time it has grown significantly to over 2,000 acres ready to explore. There are 75 camping sites that are open year-round. You will also find historic stone buildings, bridges, and tunnels that are just as beautiful and unique now as they were when originally built in the 1930s. Wildlife and bike trails abound throughout the area. There are miles of trails both paved and unpaved to travel on. This is a great camping spot for the entire family to enjoy together.

✓ How to be a best mom:

- Don't miss the playground near the Guy Park Trailhead.
- Stop by River Hills visitor center to learn about the park and pick up a souvenir from your trip.

CUIVRE RIVER

678 MO-147, Troy | 636-528-7247
mostateparks.com/park/cuivre-river-state-park

You'll camp at one of Missouri's largest state parks! Families will have a great time camping at this park that is less than an hour from St. Louis. With over 6,000 acres, there is something for everyone to enjoy at this camping spot. There's a 55-acre lake that not only has kayaking and fishing but also a beach to relax on. Those who like to hike will find an abundance of trails to choose from; Turkey Hollow Trail is on the easy side while the Cuivre River Trail will prove to be more difficult. The camping sites range from primitive to a more modern option where a canvas tent is already set up for you when you arrive.

✓ How to be a best mom:

- Keep in mind that state park representatives hold classes from the water cycle to meteor showers depending on the weekend, so contact the park to learn what programs are offered when you are there.
- Reserve a kayak before you arrive to maximize your fun.

Best Day Trip

LINCOLN SITES IN SPRINGFIELD, IL

Springfield, IL | 217-789-2360
(Visitors Center)
visitspringfieldillinois.com

You'll truly be in the Land of Lincoln! The state capital of Illinois is right at 100 miles from St. Louis and it's the perfect place for kids who like learning about presidents of the United States, particularly the 16th president. Kids will enjoy all the interactive exhibits about the life of Abraham Lincoln to be found in the presidential library and museum bearing his name. There's a well-done movie to watch in the theater that features hologram technology. Close by is the Lincoln Home for touring, and kids will think it's neat to take a stroll on the cobblestone streets. All levels of history buffs will enjoy visiting a historic village, where Lincoln lived as a young man, just outside of town in nearby New Salem. If you make it over to Lincoln's Tomb, be sure to rub the nose on his bronze head for luck.

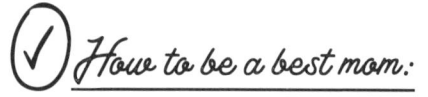

✓ How to be a best mom:

- Take the Amtrak train to Springfield for the weekend.
- Grab the original corn dog on a stick for lunch or dinner at the Cozy Dog Drive In.

ELEPHANT ROCKS STATE PARK

7406 Hwy. 21, Belleview | 573-546-3454
mostateparks.com/park/elephant-rocks-state-park

You'll climb on some granite rocks that are 1.5 billion years old! This state park is a natural playground. What at first appears to be a forest with hiking trails that is sporadically dotted with small rock formations opens up to a clearing filled with massive pink granite boulders. Kids will love climbing all over the rock formations that can heat up significantly in the sun. There are plenty of crevices and spaces between the rocks for kids to squeeze into. When it comes to hiking trails, the shorter trail around the elephant-shaped rocks is only one mile in length and it's designated as an interpretive Braille Trail where kids will enjoy trying to decipher the meaning of the signs with braille alphabet.

✓ How to be a best mom:

- Print off a bird checklist for this particular state park (found on the parks department's website) and look for the types of feathered friends in the area.
- Take some time to explore or cool off swimming in nearby Johnson's Shut-Ins State Park.

POPEYE TRAIL IN CHESTER, IL

Chester, IL | chesterill.com

You'll visit Popeye the Sailor Man! Cartoonist Elzie C. Segar was born in this small Southern Illinois town, and it's said that his work was influenced by the community. Over the years, his hometown has paid homage to his creation of Popeye by placing granite statues of the different characters throughout the city. Through generous donations and sponsorships of local businesses, these statues have been popping up all over town since 2006. To date there are more than 20 statues on the Popeye Trail, and some coordinate well with the location they are placed in. Statues of Popeye's nephews can be found in front of the local grade school, and King Blozo sits in front of City Hall. Maps are available to help you find each monument on the Popeye & Friends Character Trail, and you can use your smartphone for the QR codes found on each statue to get more information about the character.

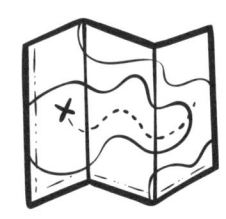

✓ How to be a best mom:

- Visit Elzie C. Segar Memorial Park to see the bronze *Popeye* statue and overlook the Mississippi River.
- Attend the town's annual fall festival.

Best Historical Place

MISSOURI HISTORY MUSEUM

5700 Lindell Blvd. | 314-746-4599 | mohistory.org/museum

You'll see the *Spirit of St. Louis* up in the air while indoors! Kids will love exploring the History Clubhouse. It's a free exhibit and truly a hidden gem within the walls of a treasured Forest Park museum. Combining play with learning from the moment you enter, you will begin in a modern downtown setup before being transported back in time through a replica trolley. The areas of local history are divided up into 1904 World's Fair, Mississippi River steamboat era, and life in ancient Cahokia Mounds. Dressing up in period clothing, pulling a steamboat whistle, pretending to fish from a wooden canoe, and serving play food in an early 20th-century café are just a few of the imaginative play opportunities.

✓ How to be a best mom:

- Attend one of the many exhibits or events (like story time) that happen throughout the year.
- Have a seat while your kids put on a puppet show. Better yet, take part in the performance.

JEFFERSON BARRACKS

345 North Rd. W | 314-615-8884
stlouiscountymo.gov/st-louis-county-departments/parks/places/jefferson-barracks-park

You'll experience US military history on the bluffs of the Mississippi River! Once an active post for the US Army from 1826 to 1946, it's not surprising that this park is on the National Register of Historic Places. Unlike typical parks, this pride of the St. Louis area is the place to experience the past. Visitors can learn about US historical events and hear stories from veterans who now volunteer in the various museums. Buildings found within this 300-plus-acre park consist of the Old Ordnance Room, Powder Magazine Museum, Laborers House and Ordnance Stable, Missouri Civil War Museum, Telephone Museum, and POW-MIA Museum, just to name a few. Families will enjoy learning together about the bygone days on a truly beautiful stretch of settlement.

✓ How to be a best mom:

- In the summer months, take a change of clothes and stop in on the splash pad in neighboring Sylvan Springs Park at 300 Halsey Rd.
- Take your kids to act out a performance on the stage of the Jefferson Barracks Veterans Memorial Amphitheater at 533 Bagby Rd.

CAHOKIA MOUNDS STATE HISTORIC SITE

30 Ramey St., Collinsville, IL | 618-346-5160
cahokiamounds.org

You'll climb just over 150 steps to reach the top of an ancient temple! Massive historical mounds can be found just a short drive across the river from downtown. This "City of the Sun" dates back to prehistoric times and was the largest settlement of Native Americans in all of North, South, and Central America. The inhabitants constructed mounds from dirt, with the largest being Monks Mound, to serve as burial places and to be used for religious ceremonies. Kids will enjoy counting the steps as they climb and exploring on the pathways around this sacred burial ground. There's also an interpretive center museum across the street from the main mounds with trails that your family will enjoy walking around to explore nature.

✓ How to be a best mom:

- Climb the 100-foot mound in the morning before it gets too sunny and hot.
- Stop by the reconstruction of Woodhenge just down the road.

35

Best Bike Trail

GRANT'S TRAIL

bikegrantstrail.com

You'll love looking over at a field of Clydesdales from your bike! This 10-mile-long bike path stretches from Kirkwood to Affton. It's flat, has well-designated crossings, and offers access to a few parks with playgrounds for when you want to take a break. There are also quite a few points of interest along the way like the Ulysses S. Grant National Historic Site, Grant's Farm, and even an area dedicated to off-road biking. Kids will love stopping by to say hello to the Clydesdales at Grant's Farm, but don't get too close or feed the horses. They will bite and there's an electric wire behind the beautiful white fencing. This great trail has it all for the entire family to enjoy a bike ride together.

✓ How to be a best mom:

- Remember your bike lock to lock up your transportation while visiting Grant's Farm.
- Stop off for a refreshment at the Sappington House Barn Restaurant.

MADISON COUNTY TRANSIT BIKE TRAILS

mcttrails.org/map.aspx

You'll bike around what was once a Valley of Coal! Part of coal mining history, the cities of Glen Carbon and Edwardsville, Illinois, are now connected by a well-kept system of trails. Miles upon miles of train track that meandered through the forest for the purpose of transporting coal have since been converted to some impressive bike trails. As you make your way through awnings of trees and open spaces, you are sure to encounter all sorts of nature. You can easily connect to the Morris Trail to explore the SIUE campus, and those up to the challenge will enjoy trying out mountain biking on the trails that go off road. With seven loops of trails overall, there are countless areas of new adventure to explore.

✓ *How to be a best mom:*

- Start your bike trip at Edwardsville Township Community Park so kids can see the restored fighter jet and play on the fun playground.
- Plan out your route for the day on the interactive trail map online.

KATY TRAIL STATE PARK

mostateparks.com/park/katy-trail-state-park

You'll bike just part of this trail at a time! This popular cycling route consists of 240 miles of trails, so it's an exploration that will take more than a few visits when kids are in tow. The trail starts just north of St. Louis and offers many opportunities for adventure along the way. As one of the longest continuous trails in the United States, it passes through many towns, big and small. There are ample amounts of bike racks in the various communities for hopping on and off the trail to take a break. Experience the charm of old Main Street St. Charles, enjoy the view from the bluffs overlooking the Missouri River in the Weldon Springs area, or stop off for lunch at one of the eateries in Defiance. There are literally miles and miles for the entire family to explore on the rails-to-trails path.

✓ *How to be a best mom:*

- Access the Katy Trail via the connector trail in Creve Coeur Park.
- Make sure to pack plenty of snacks if you are planning an extended bike ride.

fun IDEA

Best Place for the Animal Lover

LONE ELK PARK

1 Lone Elk Park Rd., Valley Park | 314-615-4386
stlouiscountymo.gov/st-louis-county-departments/parks/places/lone-elk-park

You'll experience the Western wonder of bison and elk without having to visit Yellowstone! This 546-acre animal refuge is free (but it accepts donations) and open to the public year-round. It has been wowing locals as a drive-through park since 1971. This family favorite also has quite the history. During both World War II and the Korean War, the property was used for testing and storage of ammunition. At the time, all wildlife was removed, but it's said that one lone elk mistakenly remained. When the area once again became a sanctuary for wildlife, the left-behind elk inspired the park's name. Hiking trails can be found throughout the park, and there's even an observation tower for climbing at the entrance, both of which are perfect for family nature viewing.

✓ How to be a best mom:

- Pack a lunch and enjoy eating at one of the designated picnic areas.
- Get a reservation to take the kids fishing (catch and release) at the lake.

WORLD BIRD SANCTUARY

125 Bald Eagle Ridge Rd., Valley Park | 636-225-4390
worldbirdsanctuary.org

You'll see so many bald eagles in one place! Founded in 1977, this bird rescue is conveniently located by another reserve for wildlife, Lone Elk Park. Unlike its neighbor, this conservation area is all about the avian variety of wildlife. Throughout the year there are educational programs and special events to attend. Kids will enjoy walking around the outside of large birdcage enclosures, many bigger than most residential homes. Majestic bald eagles, hawks, chickens, and inquisitive-looking barn owls are just some of the birds your family will look at in awe.

✓ How to be a best mom:

- Adopt a bird or sponsor a feathered friend in the hospital that is located on-site.
- Spend some time on the playground or take a walk through the woods on one of the hiking trails.

SUSON PARK

6073 Wells Rd.
stlouiscountymo.gov/st-louis-county-departments/parks/places/suson-park

You'll hear farm animals from the playground! Perfect for animal lovers, this park is unique and bound to become a favorite. Kids will enjoy seeing all the different animals you might find on a farm, up close and personal. This working animal farm has fence-enclosed pastures, wire pens, and outbuildings that are all filled with just about every type of farm animal. The rustic red barn houses miniature horses as well as educational information. There's a lake that is perfect for learning to fish, so don't forget to take along a fishing pole. Families can enjoy time together as they take a stroll around or over the bridge across the lake, watching geese and ducks swim by.

✓ How to be a best mom:

- Make a point of going to Suson Park Fridays to experience fun hayrides, games, and more.
- Take a remote-controlled boat along to drive on the lake.

Best Place for Educational Outdoors

MASTODON STATE HISTORIC SITE

1050 Charles J. Becker Dr., Imperial | 636-464-2976
mostateparks.com/park/mastodon-state-historic-site

You'll realize that prehistoric creatures once roamed the St. Louis area! The museum housed in this state park is free for kids and the best place to stand in awe next to an impressive 10-foot-tall mastodon skeletal replica. Other exhibits are life-scale mannequins of Native Americans depicted living alongside the American mastodon with Ice Age fossils and artifacts on display. There's an informative film shown about the site. Kids will think it's neat to see the original Kimmswick Bone Bed where the archeological discoveries were made, just a short walk down a hill. In addition to that trail, there are a few other easy trails to enjoy.

✓ How to be a best mom:

- Plan to eat a picnic lunch near the playground.
- Take along a change of clothes and shoes if the kids want to splash around in the stream that runs through the park.

HISTORIC DANIEL BOONE HOME

1868 Hwy. F, Defiance | 636-798-2005
sccmo.org/1701/The-Historic-Daniel-Boone-Home

You'll step back in time to the Missouri frontier! There's more to this site than just the interesting Boone family home built of stone blocks. The grounds hold a quaint village of buildings that were all moved to the location. Kids will enjoy seeing what life involved back in those days as they wander around structures like a mill, barn, schoolhouse, blacksmith building, general store, and many others. Take a guided tour to explore all three floors of the Boone Home or just wander outdoors on your own. A fun family activity that's also educational, there's plenty of room to run and play while going place to place in the village area.

✓ How to be a best mom:

- Check in at the office and get instructions for a fun scavenger hunt that goes through the historic village.
- Don't miss seeing the covered bridge that has been constructed off to the edge of the village.

ENDANGERED WOLF CENTER

6750 Tyson Valley Rd., Eureka | 636-938-5900
endangeredwolfcenter.org

You'll have to resist the urge to howl! For wolves to be introduced into the wild, they shouldn't look to humans as communicators. On the grounds of what was once a secret army base, this animal recovery center is all about helping to build up the endangered wolf population. Four species of wolves live in habitats on the property: red, Mexican gray, African painted, and South American maned. The red wolf is the most endangered in the world with fewer than 35 in the United States. There are also some foxes: arctic, red, swift, and African fennec. The goal for most is to reintroduce them into the wild, but there are some nonrecovery animals that will always live in the sanctuary. Families will enjoy a slow-paced tour, stopping off at the various habitats to both view and learn more about the animals.

✓ How to be a best mom:

- Peruse and find creative gifts in the shop that's housed in a World War II ammunition storage facility.
- Attend a night event when howling is allowed.

Best Place to Go Fishing

JEFFERSON LAKE
Corner of Faulkner Dr. and Clayton Ave. | 636-441-4554
mdc.mo.gov/discover-nature/places/jefferson-lake-st-louis

You'll fish in the city! Undoubtedly the best place for urban fishing in the entire area, this lake is nine acres and can be found in the southeastern corner of Forest Park. It's unusual to be able to catch a trout while listening to the hustle and bustle of a busy medical center nearby, but that's just how metropolitan this fishing spot is. There's a walking path that goes all the way around the lake and benches sporadically placed. Nothing compares to this novel place to fish.

✓ How to be a best mom:

- Follow the path across Clayton Avenue to see the Blue Angel jet and dinosaurs outside of the McDonnell Planetarium.
- Take a walk to the old fish hatchery that's located north of the lake.

VLASIS PARK

300 Park Dr., Ballwin | 636-227-8950
ballwin.mo.us/About-Our-Parks

You'll find two ponds connected by a waterfall! One pond is fully stocked and has docks with walkways that are perfect for fishing. There's even a covered dock that extends into the picturesque pond. Kids will enjoy seeing the geese meandering around the area as well as feeling the excitement of catching a fish. There are plenty of pavilions to catch some shade, and if you need to pivot activities, there's an awesome playground to explore.

✓ How to be a best mom:

- The Ballwin Days festival is held annually in the park, so check the dates each year to attend the fun.
- Look for the Little Free Library box sitting between the pond and playground and leave a book for someone else to enjoy.

BEE TREE PARK

2701 Finestown Ave. | 314-615-4386
stlouiscountymo.gov/st-louis-county-departments/parks/places/bee-tree-park

You'll fish right next to the Mississippi River! This park has so many beautiful settings to be found in its almost 200 acres. Overlooking the river is a nine-acre lake that's well stocked and a popular location for fishing. Kids will enjoy being surprised with what's caught on the end of the line, whether it's a bass, bluegill, or channel catfish. If you need to stretch your legs after fishing, there are ample trails to explore. You can also take a stroll in the Nims Mansion garden area or visit the park's playground.

✓ How to be a best mom:

- Be sure to take along a blanket or lawn chairs to sit on along the edge of the lake.
- Plan to return to take family pictures in front of the mansion, a historical landmark and unique place to visit.

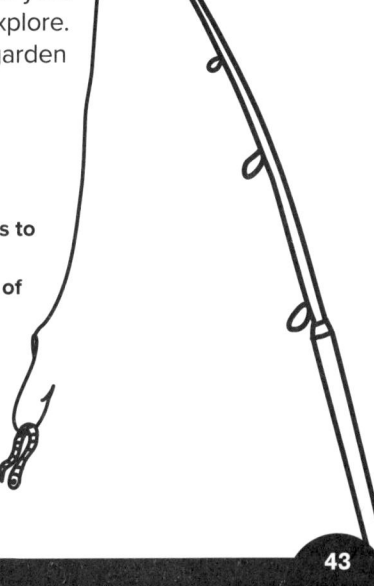

Best Fun Run

I LOVE FOREST PARK 5K AND KIDS FUN RUN

runsignup.com

You'll go for a run in the park! This run takes place not just in any park in St. Louis, but the one and only Forest Park. With an almost-six-mile path that circles the park, it's not at all uncommon to see people running around, and this fun run is a great way to introduce your kids to the recreation. The run goes by so many favorite landmarks, and you'll enjoy putting one foot in front of the other while passing the World's Fair Pavilion, art museum, zoo, and Muny. Older kids may want to sign up for the longer-distance run, while the family run is perfect for jogging or walking. Whatever your speed, there's something for the entire family and even a virtual option if you can't make it out to the park.

✓ How to be a best mom:

- After the run, make a day of the park by taking time for a cool-down stroll through the zoo or for browsing the art museum.
- Get a group of other families together to participate in the event.

TURKEY TROT

ttstl.com

You'll love getting the wiggles out before you gobble the big Thanksgiving meal! This run gathers in the morning on Thanksgiving Day and starts at the Family Arena St. Charles. It's a popular run for families due to the course being flat and different options in length. There's a 5K option participants can sign up for, a free half-mile course for kids 12 and under to enjoy, and a virtual option if you want to stay closer to home. The Turkey Trot benefits the local food pantry, and kids will love being a part of giving back by donating canned goods. Making this fun run part of your Thanksgiving holiday each year is healthy for you and the community.

✓ How to be a best mom:

- Don't forget to pick up the race swag to show off to your friends and family at dinner later that day.
- Register early to save on the entry fee.

LAURA'S RUN 4 KIDS

thelittlebitfoundation.org/events/lr4k
runsignup.com/Race/MO/SaintLouis/LaurasRun4Kids

You'll have fun, get exercise, and give back to the community all at the same time! Laura Hettiger, an Emmy Award–winning journalist, combined her love of running with a local charity to do some good. This event has become a favorite run for families and for good reason. It's no secret that Laura cares about the community she now calls home, and it shines through her enthusiasm. The Little Bit Foundation helps to supply children with clothes, food, and books. Donations also help to give assistance for children with health issues. The 5K and family fun run is held once a year and offers an option for any age, be it the 5K run, the one-mile family fun run, or the virtual option. Get a group together for a registration discount. Fun family activities, fun music, fun atmosphere, and fun sponsors make this downtown fun run one that you won't want to miss.

✓ How to be a best mom:

- Save the race shirts each year to make a quilt one day of all the fun runs your family has participated in.
- Become a fundraiser and set a goal to raise money as a family.

fun IDEA

Best Place for Geocaching

FOREST PARK

5595 Grand Dr. | 314-367-7275
forestparkforever.org

You'll find geocache stops in the most likely of places! With its vast size it's not at all surprising that Forest Park has more than a few locations for the popular outdoor activity of geocaching. While the stops are in likely places, kids will still have to hunt to find the exact locations. After all, the park itself is over 1,300 acres, and individual outdoor attractions, like the Nature Playscape, cover quite a big area. With well over 50 caches to discover, Forest Park is a great place to go back again and again for more discovery. It's a fun scavenger hunt the entire family can enjoy.

How to be a best mom:

- Go to the dollar store and let kids pick out some treasures to leave behind at a few of the designated geocache stops.
- Get a specific GPS device for geocaching or get an app on your phone.

KIRKWOOD PARK

111 S Geyer Rd., Kirkwood | 314-822-5855
kirkwoodparksandrec.org/Home/Components/FacilityDirectory/FacilityDirectory/10/444

You'll find some caches quickly! This might not be the park for creating your own caches due to the amount already in a small area, but it's the perfect place for introduction to this fun recreation. Many of the waterproof containers are easy to find, making it great to build kids' geocaching confidence when they're just starting out. Another win for this location is the opportunity in the warmer months to make even more memories while hunting for the next treasure by getting a shaved ice from the Tropical Moose right there in the same park. Overall, this park is a great place to build interest in the activity of hunting for coordinates and not overwhelming.

✓ How to be a best mom:

- Explore another type of similar outdoor recreation with St. Louis Orienteering Club events that take place periodically in the park.
- Go to Emmenegger Nature Park (also in Kirkwood) to hunt for the oldest geocache in St. Louis County.

GREAT RIVERS GREENWAY

greatriversgreenway.org

You'll travel to geocache locations by bike! This system of trails is also a great place for exploring the world of hidden treasure. The greenway connects communities and has many scenic views along the area rivers. Simply print off an online map of various geocaching coordinates that can be found along the Great Rivers Greenway and then take your GPS device of choice and start biking. Some of them are hidden in plain sight while others will be more difficult. The fun in geocaching on the greenway is that there's so much area to explore and you will be getting exercise at the same time. Take a geocache prize and leave one behind for the next person to enjoy.

✓ How to be a best mom:

- Outfit your kids with a cross-body bag that contains snacks for the journey and a pencil or pen so they can record their names in the cache's logbook.
- Create your own cache and then register the coordinates so others can find it.

Best Place to Learn All about Lewis and Clark

LEWIS & CLARK BOAT HOUSE AND MUSEUM

1050 S Riverside Dr., St. Charles
636-947-3199
lewisandclarkboathouse.org

You'll go on an elevated expedition above the banks of the Missouri River! Visitors are immediately greeted by a statue of Lewis's Newfoundland dog, Seaman, standing guard over the building. A museum adored by generations, that was once in the heart of Old St. Charles, now sits in the upper level of this rustic-looking boathouse built of stone and contrasting wood. Each year the MR340 race ends at the boathouse, making it an even more important destination. The museum is filled with historical artifacts all about the Lewis and Clark Expedition, and kids will enjoy doing the scavenger hunt that consists of identifying the various types of animals that live in the area. Tall windows look out over the river, and stepping out on the back deck affords even more of a view to watch the river flow by.

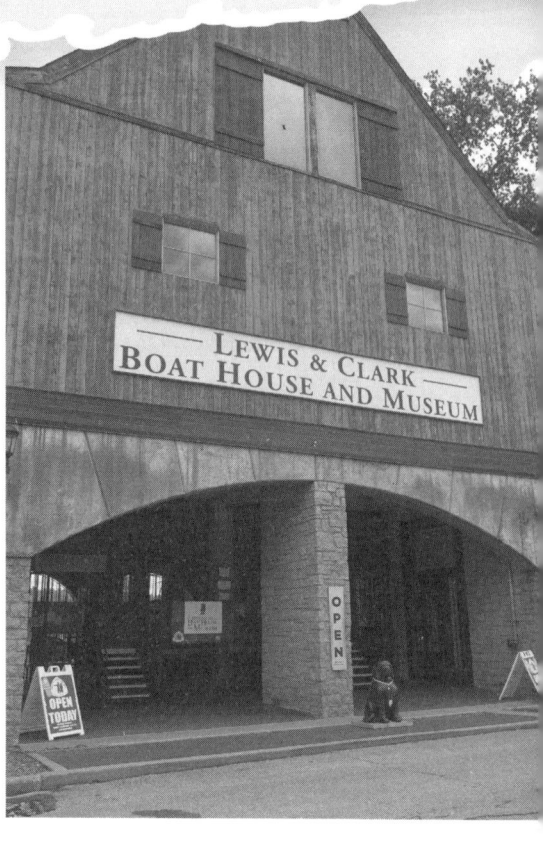

✓ How to be a best mom:

- Go to Main Street St. Charles and look around for more black dog statues of Seaman.
- Find the Forget-Me-Not Park and play a game of chess on one of the many small game tables.

EDWARD "TED" AND PAT JONES-CONFLUENCE POINT STATE PARK

1000 Riverlands Way, West Alton | 636-899-1135
mostateparks.com/park/edward-ted-and-pat-jones-confluence-point-state-park

You'll stand where two mighty rivers come together! This state park is a hidden gem with educational plaques about Lewis and Clark along with history of the indigenous peoples who lived in the area. You can easily access the piece of land that jets out into the water, with the Mississippi River running along one side and the Missouri River on the other, by taking a short walk from the parking lot. It's just under a mile there and back so not a major hike, but it's perfect for the entire family. Kids will be amazed that they are standing on the banks of two different rivers. The beach area will change from rocky to sand to mud to being covered in sticks depending on the flow of the rivers. If the riverways are high, don't be surprised if the point is completely flooded over.

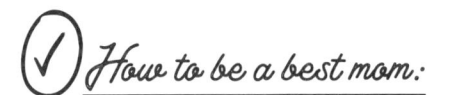

✓ How to be a best mom:

- Take a picture of one person standing on the Missouri sign inlayed in the sidewalk and another standing on the Mississippi sign.
- Travel across the bridge to Alton, Illinois, and visit the National Great Rivers Museum.

LEWIS & CLARK LIBRARY BRANCH

9909 Lewis and Clark Blvd. | 314-994-3300
slcl.org/hours-and-locations/lewis-clark-branch

You'll read in a canoe! Where better to feel connected to the Lewis and Clark Expedition than in a library located on Lewis and Clark Boulevard in a branch named after them? The previous library on this site featured beautiful stained glass designed by artist Robert Harmon depicting the journey of Meriwether Lewis and William Clark, complete with Sacajawea. These three stained glass windows, at the request of the Moline Acres community, were included in the new St. Louis County Library that opened on the spot in 2015. Kids will love seeing the light shine through the colorful glass and sitting in one of the two replica canoes for the expedition in the children's area of the library. There are also occasional displays highlighting the history of the Lewis and Clark Expedition, so watch for those throughout the year.

✓ How to be a best mom:

- Check out some books about Lewis and Clark to either read in the canoe or take home.
- Sign up for an event or activity that is held at this library branch.

Best Farmers Market

TOWER GROVE FARMERS' MARKET

Tower Grove Park | Center Cross Dr.
tgfarmersmarket.com

You'll come across a farmers market that is a walk in the park! More than 100 vendors can be found selling everything from farm-fresh eggs and produce to local honey, baked goods, and so much more. Many booths have fresh flowers and plants for sale as well. There are even vegetable plants to start your own garden at home. Locally made soaps, jewelry, and other handmade wares line the pathways of this community favorite. You can also enjoy food items being prepared fresh from area merchants. The overall vibe is even more energetic with local musicians performing in the park, and kids will enjoy dancing around to the music. It's truly a local shopping experience that the entire family can be part of.

✓ *How to be a best mom:*

- Take your kids to the playground and splash pad just steps away from the vendor booths.
- Pick out something adventurous to snack on in the shade of the Turkish Pavilion.

SOULARD FARMERS MARKET

730 Carroll St. | 314-622-4180
soulardmarketstl.com

You'll shop in the oldest farmers market west of the Mississippi! While the open-air concept for this market began in 1779, the current location has been in operation since 1838. Kids will love the lively atmosphere of this market as they hear merchants yelling out sale prices. The indoor market is open year-round and the place to find all things fresh. In summer months there are even more vendor booths located in the open space outside of the market. The entire family will enjoy seeing all the fresh produce, meats, pasta, bakery items, and so much more at this urban staple of the community.

✓ How to be a best mom:

- Go by the Harr Family Farms booth to feed the chickens and pet the other animals that may make an appearance.
- Watch some mini donuts being made, which have been a part of Soulard Market for generations.

KIRKWOOD FARMERS' MARKET

150 E Argonne Dr., Kirkwood | 314-984-9496
thesummitkirkwood.com

You'll think you are at a farm fruit stand, but bigger! This farmers market is right in historic downtown Kirkwood, a suburban community that still has a small-town feel. From the outside it looks like an oversized produce stand, and inside there's everything from fresh produce to cheeses and local honey. There's even a boutique section to find one-of-a-kind gifts and a well-stocked garden center. Kids will really enjoy the seasonal traditions throughout the year like picking out the best carving pumpkin and perfect holiday tree.

✓ How to be a best mom:

- In the summer months, plan on getting a shaved ice treat from the Tropical Moose on the edge of the market.
- Go in the fall for the Great Pumpkin Patch Kids Fall Fun Zone and at Christmastime for the Gingerbread Shoppe.

Best Pick-Your-Own Farm

ECKERT'S

951 S Green Mt. Rd., Belleville, IL
618-310-2758 | eckerts.com

You'll pick your own produce right from the tree, vine, or bush! With three Eckert's locations (all of which have apple orchards), St. Louisans have been making the trip just over the river into Illinois for generations to pick their own apples. It's a family tradition that has evolved over time to include all sorts of pick-your-own seasonal items. From many varieties of apples and strawberries to peaches, raspberries, and blackberries, this family farm system is one that dates back to the late 1800s. Each location has different fun farm activities and events that the entire family will enjoy, particularly in the fall. Kids especially love being able to pick out their own pumpkin for carving, and the apple cider donuts are an absolute must. Wagon rides, bonfires, live music, and so much more round out this fantastic farm adventure.

✓ *How to be a best mom:*

- Let the kids pick out a mouthwatering pie to order for your holiday dinner.
- Go on a weekend road trip to the Eckert's in Versailles, Kentucky.

THIES FARM AND MARKET

3200 Greens Bottom Rd., St. Charles | 636-447-2230
thiesfarm.com

You'll be impressed where you find farmland! Nestled in between Creve Coeur and St. Charles is a true farm that's not at all far from a populated area. This fifth-generation farm started out on Hanley Road clear back in 1885 so it has quite the history in the St. Louis area. Every season yields different pickable produce. From strawberries in the spring to blackberries and raspberries in the summer months, kids will love filling their own bucket with fresh fruit. There's even often a field set aside for planting sunflowers and zinnias that can be freshly picked by you in the summer. In the fall, pumpkins are the choice pick, and the Pumpkinland activities are a favorite. Kids of all ages will enjoy the corn maze, hay bale tunnels, and so much more.

✓ How to be a best mom:

- Organize a fundraiser selling Thies potted plants and hanging baskets for your kids' school.
- Pick up some local honey that's a great help for allergies.

TANGLED TINSEL CHRISTMAS TREE FARM

5 Christmas Tree Ln., Alton, IL | 618-465-7036 | grifarm.com

You'll cut your own Christmas tree! For over 13 years this tree farm, with its small-farm feel and picturesque hills, has been a favorite for families. The first Saturday of December is dedicated to a free event with Santa, and one cup of hot chocolate is always free in the gift shop. While you will find a larger variety in types of precut trees available, it's the choose-your-own that has the hearts of many. There's no entry fee, and across five acres you will find around 400 trees of white pine and fir types ranging in height from six to 10 feet. Simply pick out the tree that will look stunning in your home, use the provided saw, and cut. The trees take seven to 10 years to grow, so three trees are planted per every one cut. Kids will love the fun of finding just the right tree and bringing the fresh pine smell into their home.

✓ How to be a best mom:

- Call your favorite photographer and then book a session through Tangled Tinsel for holiday photos.
- Get some friends together and register for a wreath-making party at the farm.

Best Ways to Volunteer

Courtesy of Lisa Rivera

ST. LOUIS AREA FOODBANK

70 Corporate Woods Dr., Bridgeton | 314-292-6262 | stlfoodbank.org

You'll work together in teams to fight hunger! By letting you register online for a time slot, this organization makes volunteering an easy process. Once you arrive at the food bank for your assigned time, workers explain everything you need to know for completing your task and are helpful along the way. Everyone is happy and has a common goal of helping others. There's a job for all ages and abilities. Assignments while volunteering at the food bank include unboxing donated household supplies, sorting canned goods to check expiration dates, and packing boxes of food to be sent to area shelters or food pantries. Volunteering at this food bank is a great way to introduce the entire family to just how easy it is to make a difference in the community.

✓ How to be a best mom:

- Get a group of friends to sign up with you and then spend a Saturday morning volunteering together.
- Donate $50 to the food bank to help feed a family for two weeks.

COOL!

JUSTSERVE

justserve.org

You'll discover all sorts of ways to volunteer! This free app makes it easy to find opportunities to serve others. Searching by zip code, you can find local projects right where you live or in the surrounding areas. There's sure to be a listing that all ages can be involved in, making this the perfect source for ideas for families. Help to clean up a cemetery, prepare and deliver a lasagna to someone in need, or just be a friend to someone who has sought refuge in St. Louis. There are so many opportunities that kids can take part in.

✓ How to be a best mom:

- Instead of going to a playground, look for one that you can help clean up.
- Ask your kids what type of service they'd like to do so they are involved in the decision.

great idea!

LITTLE FREE LIBRARY

littlefreelibrary.org

You'll create a library in your own neighborhood! Building and maintaining a Little Free Library is a great way to stay connected with your neighbors. It gives kids a sense of accomplishment and responsibility. This entire volunteer project is relatively easy to do. Kids will enjoy being involved in the planning from beginning to end, especially choosing the paint colors and overall design. To get started simply identify where you would like to have your library box located (many people choose their front yard by the sidewalk), build a box using plans found online (or purchase a ready-made box), register your little library, and then fill it with books. It's a project for the entire family to be involved in together and a fun way to give back while encouraging your kids with the importance of reading.

✓ How to be a best mom:

- Donate books to the Greater St. Louis Book Fair.
- Give to the Little Free Pantry that's attached to the Little Free Library located at 11735 Denny Rd.

55

Best Place to Read a Book

JEWEL BOX

Intersection of Wells and McKinley Drives | 314-531-0080
stlouis-mo.gov/government/departments/parks/parks/Jewel-Box.cfm

You'll fall in love with the gem of Forest Park! Constructed in 1936, the Jewel Box is a perfect example of the art deco era. The historic glass atrium filled with exotic plants is indeed the crown jewel, but the surrounding area is just as fun to explore. There are so many quiet areas for sitting down with a good book, whether you choose to read on a bench or under a tree. Depending on the time of year, varying types of plants and flowers will be surrounding the reflection pool. Several intertwining pathways are perfect for taking an enjoyable stroll around the grounds if the kids need a break from reading.

✓ How to be a best mom:

- Take a picnic lunch and let the kids explore the area on their own.
- Be sure to come in the spring and take family pictures when the tulips are in bloom.

Courtesy of Don Korte

56

FRONTIER PARK

500 S Riverside Dr.
stcharlesparks.com/park/frontier-park

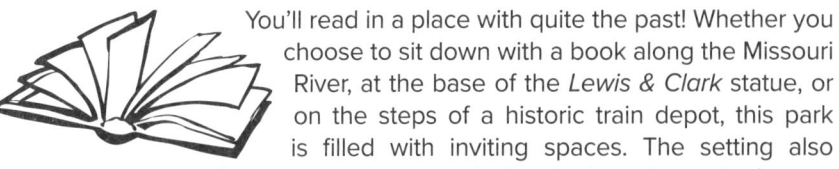

You'll read in a place with quite the past! Whether you choose to sit down with a book along the Missouri River, at the base of the *Lewis & Clark* statue, or on the steps of a historic train depot, this park is filled with inviting spaces. The setting also provides the perfect opportunity to read a book about the region's past, bringing history to life. Kids are especially sure to enjoy reading stories of the Native Americans who lived in the area or about the expedition that included the black dog, Seaman, on Lewis and Clark's journey. This expansive park is pleasant and relaxing for the entire family to enjoy.

✓ How to be a best mom:

- Go across the street to grab a treat from Bike Stop Café.
- Attend Festival of the Little Hills or a food truck event in the park.

MAYPOP COFFEE & GARDEN SHOP

803 Marshall Ave., Webster Groves | 314-764-2140
maypopshop.com

You'll feel like you are reading a book in an old house, because you are! This coffee shop is more than meets the eye. Outdoors is a garden shop with all sorts of beautiful plants. Inside there is a café with rooms that are sectioned off much like its time as a residence. The vintage decor and setup of each room truly have one feeling right at home. There are wall racks of lending books shelved in the entry hallway for kids to enjoy, so this is a place for all ages to sit down and read a book. Grab a pastry from the coffee bar and have a seat with book in hand next to the fireplace in the front room or on the stately front porch. There's also seating on the back porch overlooking the garden area that's a wonderful place to get your reading on.

✓ How to be a best mom:

- Let kids pick out an indoor or outdoor plant to take home.
- Stop by Margaret Atalanta Park (that's right around the corner) to enjoy the playground.

Best Place to Buy a Book

THE NOVEL NEIGHBOR

7905 Big Bend Blvd., Webster Groves | 314-738-9384
thenovelneighbor.com

You'll fall in love with the bookstore that has a neighborhood feel! The various rooms of this store feel like a home with loads of charm. Beyond the darling children's book nook and extensive collection for young adults and early to middle readers, there are book clubs for the entire family. You can enroll your little book lover in summer camp or host a birthday party in one of two different event spaces. Author visits and events are a routine occurrence as is evident by the eclectic decor on the walls: painted red squares with signatures and vintage keys attached. Each author is given the opportunity to pick out a "key to the store" that speaks to them and then write a message. See if you can find your favorite author's handwriting!

✓ *How to be a best mom:*

- Surprise your kids with either a monthly book subscription or a mystery box.
- Get your child a signed book that has been left behind by one of the visiting authors.

Feels like a home with loads of charm.

THE BOOK HOUSE

7352 Manchester Rd., Maplewood | 314-968-4491
bookhousestl.com

You'll be greeted by a suit of armor and in awe of the wall-to-wall books! With about half the books new and half used, this bookstore has it all. The rare and out-of-print books are particularly fun to look at. Sliding library ladders are functional and add to the overall atmosphere. The shop itself is just as delightful as it is impressive. As you begin the descent downstairs (where the children's books as well as an extensive area of bargain books are housed), see if you can spot the little illustrated mouse reading a book. The staircase walls are also covered with signatures of past visiting authors and a quote-filled tree mural.

✓ *How to be a best mom:*

- Be on the lookout for the cats who live among the books.
- Grab a treat at Blissfully Popped Popcorn located on the same block.

MAIN STREET BOOKS

307 S Main St., St. Charles | 636-949-0105
mainstreetbooks.net

You'll step from a cobblestone street into a true brick-and-mortar! Multiple levels of reading splendor await you right on Main Street in historic St. Charles, and one might wonder about the stories from days gone by that are within the brick walls. In business for over 30 years, the building that now holds this bookshop is a historic landmark as it once housed the office of a Missouri Secretary of State in the 1820s. Kids will find a section of books for their age range either on an upper landing of the first floor or up a longer flight of stairs to the second floor. Upon reaching the top of the stairs, all are greeted by whimsical flying keys, the perfect invitation to explore the books for young adults and middle-grade readers. Fun family events throughout the year and book clubs for teens make this the perfect destination in a popular tourist spot.

✓ *How to be a best mom:*

- Teach your kids how books are shelved and then go on a book hunt for a specific book.
- Step across the street to Kilwins for a dish of ice cream.

Best Library for Kids

KIRKWOOD PUBLIC LIBRARY

140 E Jefferson Ave., Kirkwood
314-821-5770
kirkwoodpubliclibrary.org

You'll enter a historic building that once housed a city hall and is now filled with books! The basement of this library is all about kids with a perfect mix of education, imagination, technology, and fun. Children will enjoy sitting down with a book in one of the many reading nooks. There are even spaces to read on the play train engine and caboose. Fun events abound all year long with the most popular being the monthly scavenger hunt and of course the amazing summer reading program where kids can earn prizes.

✓ How to be a best mom:

- Fill your home library with previously read children's books available for purchase at the Books & Beyond store connected to the library.
- Enroll in the family book club.

Kids can earn prizes with the reading program!

DANIEL BOONE BRANCH—ST. LOUIS COUNTY LIBRARY

300 Clarkson Rd., Ellisville | 314-994-3300
slcl.org/hours-and-locations/daniel-boone-branch

You'll discover a whole lot more than just books! The children's area in the basement of this massive library is appropriately called the Discovery Zone. It's filled with activity stations that cultivate skills like building vocabulary, creative thinking, imaginative play, problem-solving, phonics, and cause and effect. Colorful carpet tiles are sporadically placed throughout the basement, and each activity has a corresponding children's book recommendation. It's not often that you find a library complete with a slide, a playhouse, tunnels, and other fun nooks to read in, but this one has it all.

✓ How to be a best mom:

- Fill your calendar with any number of the fun events and activities throughout the year, including a fantastic summer reading program.
- Experience special Whiskers and Tales evenings where kids can practice reading to some four-legged friends from Love on a Leash.

MERAMEC VALLEY BRANCH—ST. LOUIS COUNTY LIBRARY

1501 San Simeon Way, Fenton | 314-994-3300
slcl.org/hours-and-locations/meramec-valley-branch

You'll find an enclosed children's area that combines fun with reading! If you have a runner then this library is the one for you. While the door to the glass wall is not on an alarm and doesn't lock, it is an extra way to delay a child from being able to quickly exit the room. Children will love stepping foot inside the ginormous playhouse, playing with a smaller version of a pneumatic tube, and racing timed cars down a track. They can even build a wall of bricks as they pick out some really great reads. Step out onto the covered patio to enjoy a snack from the vending machine.

✓ How to be a best mom:

- Either before or after checking out books, take a stroll on the walking path that goes around the perimeter of the library grounds.
- Get on the list to rent a spot in the community garden.

Best Place to Get a Frozen Treat

ICES PLAIN & FANCY

2256 S 39th St. | 314-601-3604
icesplainandfancy.com

You'll get the freshest ice cream in town! It's not just ice cream, it's an experience. Kids will love watching their dessert made right in front of them. From watching the mixing of the ingredients to the flame of the blowtorches and smoke from the liquid nitrogen, this ice cream experience is the coolest around. The flavors are rich and delectable. Kids will love getting their treat in a house-made waffle cone—after all, St. Louis is home to the original ice cream cone. Ices is also all about shopping local as is evident by the supplier of the milk. Think farm-to-table in the form of dessert with the main ingredient coming from a dairy farm in Greenville, Illinois. This is sure to become a place in the Shaw neighborhood you'll want to visit again and again.

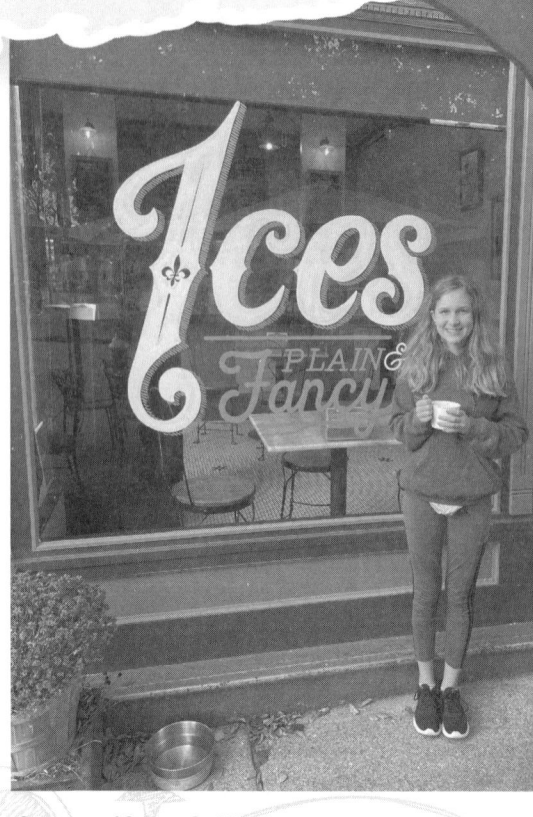

Courtesy of Steven Smith

✓ How to be a best mom:

- Get adventurous with a seasonal flavor, always for a limited time while supplies last.
- Take a pint of ice cream home with you.

Kids will love getting their treat in a house-made waffle cone!

TED DREWES

6726 Chippewa St. | 314-481-2652
teddrewes.com

You'll fall in love with this classic favorite over and over again! For over 80 years, frozen custard has put St. Louis on the map. The frozen concrete creation is thicker than a shake and can literally be turned upside down without coming out of its cup. With long-standing names like Fox Treat, Dottie, Dutchman, Crater Copernicus, and other delicious flavors, it's no wonder that the creamy frozen custard has remained popular over the generations. For many families it's also part of the holiday traditions along with picking out a Christmas tree from the frozen custard stand's own tree lot.

✓ How to be a best mom:

- In the fall, enjoy the seasonal Great Pumpkin custard treat and then watch the Charlie Brown special with a similar name at home.
- During December, bundle up warm, grab a frozen custard, and stroll down the Candy Cane Lane Christmas light display (just a few streets over on Murdoch Avenue).

CLEMENTINE'S NAUGHTY & NICE CREAMERY

140 W Argonne Dr., Kirkwood | 314-530-7600
clementinescreamery.com

You'll catch some deliciously unique ice cream flavors! This is the perfect place to go after a kids sports game. With multiple locations, this delectable small-batch creamery has quickly made a name for itself. The location in downtown Kirkwood is particularly fun, housed in the old historic Custard Station (next to the train station) and is quite a joy to experience. Ice cream is sold in scoops or pints, and hopefully a train will go by while you are visiting, because kids will love waving at the engineer to see if the train horn will sound.

✓ How to be a best mom:

- Check the train schedule to see when a train will be coming through.
- Take your four-legged family member because there's special Doggie ice cream.

63

Best Place for a Celebratory Treat

FITZ'S

fitzsrootbeer.com

You'll celebrate with a giant root beer float! Or whatever type of float suits your fancy. This soda brewery is all about combining any of their delicious fizzy drink flavors with ice cream. Getting a free float when you purchase a meal on your birthday at this restaurant makes it the perfect place to party. Kids will love the fun names like Cookie Monster, Grape Escape, Trolley Car, and Gooey Louie, and trying out the different flavor combinations each time they go. Whether you are visiting the location in the Loop or the one in South County, it's not just a float, it's a dessert.

✓ How to be a best mom:

- At the Delmar location, walk along the stars of the St. Louis Walk of Fame.
- Check the schedule to find out when you can see soda being bottled on the production line.

It's not just a float, it's a dessert.

THE FOUNTAIN ON LOCUST

3037 Locust St. | 314-535-7800
fountainonlocust.com

You'll marvel at the high-flying murals on the walls! And the specialty ice cream is quite marvelous too. Everything about this eatery is art deco. From the swanky red curtains tied back at the booths on the west side of the room to the vintage black and white tiles, you'll feel like you are in a 1920s Manhattan jazz club.

Kids will feel celebrated at the fancy establishment with the sensational sundaes. The Three Coins in the Fountain is a family favorite and big enough to be shared. There's something for everyone to enjoy, from plain ice cream to scoops with delectable toppings.

✓ *How to be a best mom:*

- Have the kids pick out a bonbon candy from the glass case at the end of the vintage soda fountain bar.
- Make a reservation (on a weekday) so there's a table or booth ready for you.

FEDERHOFER'S BAKERY

9005 Gravois Rd., Affton | 314-832-5116
federhofersbakery.com

You'll smell baked sweetness in the air! Drivers on Gravois are often filled with warm memories when they see the neon sign of the baker holding a birthday cake. With baked goods that evoke so many feelings of family traditions and childhood, you know there's bound to be quite a few different types of celebratory treats to choose from. For over 57 years this bakery has been a community favorite. Whether it's celebrating with doughnuts for a special breakfast or being rewarded with a decorated cookie, kids will love picking out the treat from the glass display cases. Custom birthday cakes can be found here, and there are even large specialty cupcakes with various iced toppings that are perfect for celebrations.

✓ *How to be a best mom:*

- Go at Christmastime and pick up a tray of traditional Christmas cookies.
- Head to play at Mathilda-Welmering Park just down the street at 8301 Mathilda Rd.

Best Theme Restaurant

PIECES BOARD GAME BAR & CAFE

1535 S 8th St. | 314-230-5184
stlpieces.com

You'll play with your food! Located just across the street from historic Soulard Farmers Market, this eclectic and fun eatery is filled with board games of all kinds. From strategy to party to classic games, your family will enjoy this spot. The venue's library of curated games is valued at over $21,000. Even ordering from the menu or asking a question is part of the game with a system at each table to grab your server's attention. Don't be shy about asking how a game is played since collectively the staff is knowledgeable about 90 percent of the games. You can sit indoors or outside on a patio with picnic tables. It's fun for the entire family and will quickly become a favorite.

✓ How to be a best mom:

- Introduce your kids to a classic game that you loved playing in childhood.
- Be sure to play the trivia game about Pieces on the front of the menu.

A fun eatery filled with board games of all kinds.

CARDINALS NATION

601 Clark St. | 314-345-9880
mlb.com/cardinals/cardinals-nation

You'll sing "Take Me Out to the Ball Game" the minute you walk in! This restaurant in Ballpark Village is the closest to the field without being in the stadium. It's also where you can get a ballpark hot dog or brat without going to the game. The theme is baseball, from chandeliers made of wood bats to jerseys framed on the walls. Kids will get a kick out of the baseball floor tiles in the restrooms. Just outside the restaurant is a green turf area with picnic tables where you can watch the televised game or play lawn games. Family night for kids to eat free, a little-league lineup of eats on the kids menu, and dining alongside memorabilia of champions make this the place for families to eat while watching the game on the big screen.

✓ How to be a best mom:

- Plan a time to visit the museum.
- Go to the steps outside with the words of the baseball song on them, sing the song with your kids, and take advantage of a great photo op.

STAGE LEFT GRILLE

541 N Grand Blvd., Ste. 1006 | 314-534-2720
fabulousfox.com/visit/stage-left-grille

You'll drool over the food and the *Playbill* posters on the walls! While this themed eatery is only open on Fabulous Fox Theatre show days, it's the place to go before attending that family musical you have tickets for. In this restaurant set up like a bougie 1950s diner, kids will request to sit in one of the comfortable booths or at the soda-fountain-looking bar. It's recommended to arrive two hours before showtime to ensure you can enjoy your meal with time to spare. The menu items are divided into Broadway-sounding terms like salads as the Opening Act, appetizer Spotlights, and Center Stage burgers. Go with a Showstopper if you are looking for something even more foodie. The entire family will like the shoestring fries and enjoying a night out at this fabulous restaurant.

✓ How to be a best mom:

- Go for lunch before a matinee on the weekend.
- Be sure to save room for one of the Fab shakes.

Best Place to Take Picky Eaters

9 MILE GARDEN

9375 Gravois Rd., Affton | 314-390-2806
9milegarden.com

You'll experience a unique dining experience outside! There's something at this food truck court that will please just about everyone. Local food trucks cook up some cuisine that you will only find in St. Louis. There's a rotating schedule that gives variety to the food options. Drinks are available in either the indoor Cantina or at an outdoor booth. Find and follow 9 Mile Garden on social media to see which trucks will be serving up food that day. There's also rotating entertainment (trivia night, live music, etc.) and yard games to play while watching a movie or sporting event on the big screen. Picky eaters will enjoy choosing from the various food trucks, and it's a fun atmosphere for the entire family.

How to be a best mom:

- Look at the food truck business menus online to get an idea of the food options for better planning.
- Check the calendar for the entertainment options for the evening.

Enjoy a unique dining experience outside!

CITY FOUNDRY STL

3730 Foundry Way
cityfoundrystl.com

You'll experience multiple restaurants in one! This is most definitely the haven for picky eaters because there's sure to be something to satisfy every appetite. Think of it as multiple small eateries within one big venue. With 15-plus kitchens, there are so many options to decide on. There are even dessert stops for ice cream or cheesecake. From pizza, burgers, and waffles to more exotic options like poke bowls, you can drop in at various times of day for lunch, dinner, or a late breakfast. This food hall is also a fun place to spend a unique snack time. With ample amounts of tables and cute nooks for hanging out, this all-in-one place is sure to become a family favorite.

✓ How to be a best mom:

- Some kitchens offer online ordering for faster service.
- Stop by one of the many shops located nearby, or play a round of mini golf at the Puttshack.

THE OLD SPAGHETTI FACTORY

727 N 1st St. | 314-621-0276
osf.com/location/st-louis-mo

You'll land in an old-world Italian restaurant on the Landing! Located in a historic part of the city, this place is all about atmosphere. Antique lighting, posh furniture, and dark wood abound. Kids will love having the ability to choose a meal to fit their own palate as noodles are available with different types of sauce, butter, or even plain. Everyone gets a three-course meal, so picky kids will feel like they have control over each step of the feast. Dessert comes in the form of either vanilla or spumoni ice cream, so kids even get to make that choice. Generations have been enjoying this pasta fare and for good reason.

✓ How to be a best mom:

- Tell the kids to eat their pasta until they find Wally the Trolley at the bottom of the bowl.
- Eat at a table in the old-fashioned trolley.

Best Place to Take an Out-of-Towner to Eat

BOATHOUSE AT FOREST PARK

6101 Government Dr. | 314-366-1555
boathousestl.com

You'll eat dinner in the middle of a world-renowned park! It's not uncommon to hear live music as you drive by this unique establishment. The restaurant in Forest Park features unique offerings from St. Louis favorite Sugarfire as well as the opportunity to hear other local favorites playing tunes to the side of the patio. Located between the Muny and World's Fair Pavilion, it's truly a hidden gem that's also a great option for taking out-of-town visitors. Whether you choose dining lakeside on the patio or indoors, it's a casual atmosphere that's perfect with food offerings for the entire family.

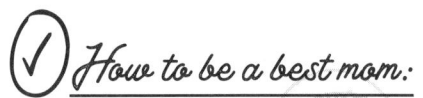

✓ How to be a best mom:

- Sit on the patio so the kids can watch the ducks walking around the docks or swimming by on the water.
- Rent a paddleboat before or after your meal.

It's truly a hidden gem!

CUNETTO HOUSE OF PASTA

5453 Magnolia Ave. | 314-781-1135
cunetto.com

You'll eat on The Hill! In the heart of the area of St. Louis that is known for Italian meals, this restaurant is a family tradition for so many locals and for good reason. Everything about this establishment is inviting, making it the perfect place to introduce your out-of-town visitors to authentic Italian cuisine. Even the dining room will have you thinking you are eating at an Italian grandmother's house. The food with names all in Italian is amazing, and the casual atmosphere is great for kids to dine with the rest of the family.

✓ How to be a best mom:

- Dinner service starts are 4:45 p.m. and it's a long-standing policy not to take reservations, so try to arrive early.
- Introduce kids to a dish of spumoni ice cream for dessert or take a cannoli home for later.

IMO'S PIZZA

imospizza.com

You'll share the "square beyond compare"! With various locations all over the area, you are sure to find this Provel-covered pizza close to you. Aside from the square-cut slices, the unique cheese topping is what sets this pizza pie apart from others. Even the salad has a flavor all its own. For generations this has been the chosen pizza for St. Louisans to serve at sports parties or kids' birthday slumber parties. Professional athletes have been known to have the pizza shipped to their new location after being traded out of the area. The eat-in restaurants are laid back and the perfect place for having kids in tow while introducing your out-of-town guests to the St. Louis favorite pizza.

✓ How to be a best mom:

- Get an order of traditional St. Louis toasted ravioli.
- Pick up a pizza and enjoy it at your favorite local park.

Best Place for the Little Carnivore

HI-POINTE DRIVE-IN

1033 McCausland Ave. | 314-349-2720
hipointedrivein.com

You'll show up for the burgers and enjoy the eclectic charm! There are multiple locations to choose from, all with their own varying reasons to visit. Kids will think it's fun to dine in an outdoor shipping crate at the location next to the historic Hi-Pointe Theatre, and if you want something quick or on the go, the Kirkwood location has a pickup window. With all the unique combinations, this burger joint is more than just the typical roadside drive-in. Kids will enjoy dressing up their own burger with the different sauces. Add some fries or the special milkshake of the week alongside the all-beef patty for a meal that is both family friendly and sure to become a quick favorite.

✓ How to be a best mom:

- Visit Sugarfire for a barbecue establishment that is part of the same company.
- Download the app and be rewarded on your birthday.

PAPPY'S SMOKEHOUSE

3106 Olive St. | 314-535-4340
pappyssmokehouse.com

You'll have Memphis-style barbecue in St. Louis! What makes this place famous, in addition to the mouthwatering eats, is the simplicity of it all. Simply walk in, stand in line, order your food at the counter, and then find a table in this industrial-looking venue. Kids will like pairing the numerous homemade sauces with their meal or trying different fixings on the side. When it comes to cleanup there's no need to worry if you have a messy little eater because you'll find a roll of paper towels on every table. This entire setting is low key and perfect for families to enjoy a meal together.

✓ How to be a best mom:

- The smoked goodness does take hours to make, so go early, because once the barbecue runs out, it's out.
- Pick up some merch and take some of that popular sauce home.

SALT + SMOKE

314-727-0200 | saltandsmokebbq.com

You'll combine St. Louis famous toasted ravioli with Southern barbecue! With seven locations (and growing), you won't have to look far to find slow-smoked brisket close to home. All locations are family friendly and loaded with great eating options for everyone to enjoy. There are even quick-service eat-in locations housed within the Crestwood and Kirkwood Schnucks grocery stores. Kids will get a kick out of their own menu addressed to little cowboys and cowgirls. Options abound: whether it's the world-famous brisket, pulled pork, chicken, or delectable sides, all will enjoy the portions that are big enough for leftovers.

✓ How to be a best mom:

- Do online ordering, pick up, and head to a local park for a barbecue feast.
- Try one of the suburb locations if the Loop or downtown locations are looking to be busy, particularly if there's a game in town.

Best Breakfast

THE SHACK

eatatshack.com

You'll read the writing on the wall! The walls and tables of this popular spot are covered in signatures and messages left by patrons. Kids will think it's cool to leave their mark with a Sharpie from the hostess stand. Breakfast and brunch items like waffles, omelets, biscuits and gravy, loaded hash browns, and skillet meals all have interesting names on the menu and will have you thinking about them for weeks after. Kids will love picking out two items found on their own 'Lil Shackaroos section of the menu. With five locations in the region, there's undoubtedly a Shack near you.

✓ How to be a best mom:

- The paper crowns aren't just for birthdays, so grab one for your child to wear as king or queen of the breakfast table.
- Try out lunch at the Shack or the Corner Pub & Grill owned by the same restaurant group.

UNCLE BILL'S

3427 S Kingshighway Blvd. | 314-832-1973

You'll eat a pancake the size of your head! For over 60 years this establishment has been known as the first pancake house in the city, and despite what it's known for, there are more than just stacks of fluffy flapjacks served here. Other breakfast foods like waffles, omelets, biscuits and gravy, loaded hash browns, and skillet meals are also on the extensive menu. The restaurant building itself is a unique experience with Tudor-style stucco and dark wood exterior with awnings, British pub-type decor of stained glass, and booths perfect for families. There's even a beautiful fireplace with European old-world-flair tile and sketches on the walls featuring St. Louis landmarks.

✓ How to be a best mom:

- Surprise your kids with ice cream for breakfast by ordering the Chocolate Alaska pancakes.
- Go in the evening and eat breakfast for dinner.

THE BARN

1015 Sappington Rd. | 314-966-8387
crestwoodbarn.com

You'll eat breakfast in a barn! This Crestwood barn is located on the property of the historic Old Sappington House, and it's the perfect place to appreciate breakfast. There's a flavorful menu to choose from with items that are geared toward foodies and ones that are more simplistic. The Barn Browns, their own version of hash browns, are a fan favorite, and kids will think it's neat to be able to have cinnamon, honey, butter, or maple butter topping for pancakes. Kids are also sure to like the french toast or get more adventurous with the quiche of the day. There's something for the entire family to enjoy eating in this rustically decorated venue.

✓ How to be a best mom:

- Tour the Sappington House Museum to learn about the history before the city of Crestwood existed.
- Take a walk on Grant's Trail running alongside and then continue the outdoor experience with breakfast on the patio.

75

Best Place to Learn to Get Cooking

SWEETOLOGY

2550 State Hwy. K, Hutchings Farm Shopping Plaza, O'Fallon
636-409-1123 | sweetology.com

You'll have a really sweet time together! The shop itself is eye catching with jars and tall tubes filled with candy decorating the space. There are tables for crafting bakery sensations as well as plush photo-op furniture. Kids will love decorating cakes, cupcakes, and cookies using colorful sprinkles, candies, and a rainbow of icing hues. There are even classes all about royal icing to really take your cookies to the next level. From special holiday events to birthday parties, there's so much to explore in the world of sweets at Sweetology. There's even special Nailed It Cake Competition events to have fun together while testing your skill. In addition to the classes, there are plenty of decorating kits that you can purchase and take home.

Courtesy of Sweetology

✓ How to be a best mom:

- Check out the Sweetology YouTube channel for more decorating ideas and tips.
- Order a gingerbread house decorating kit to do at home.

76

SCHNUCKS COOKING SCHOOL

12332 Manchester Rd., Des Peres | 314-909-1704
nourish.schnucks.com/web-ext/cooking-school

You'll cook with the experts! Who better to trust with your learning to cook than the place that provides the ingredients? For over 15 years this cooking school has been in the Des Peres Schnucks location. They offer fun themes that are also educational, like preparing foods that were part of the 1904 World's Fair and cookie decorating. Families will also enjoy attending classes that are devoted to pizza making and cupcakes. Kids will really enjoy the holiday-themed classes for making Halloween and Christmas cookies or celebrating with a birthday party cooking class. There are even summer camps of various lengths and for different age groups.

How to be a best mom:

- Sign kids up for the popular Competition Cooking Camps in the summer.
- Pick out a recipe with your kids and go into Schnucks together to get the ingredients so you are doing it all from start to finish.

KITCHEN CONSERVATORY

9011 Manchester Rd. | 314-862-2665
kitchenconservatory.com

You'll learn so many new recipes! In addition to on-site classes, this cooking school has an entire catalog of recipes you can purchase online. The classes that are specially created for kids are popular and sell out quickly. These cooking classes are also designed to be taken with your kids, so it's a great way to bond over the food. From themes that offer a wizarding good time to thrilling pastas and pizzas, there are plenty of options to expand on a child's love of cooking or just to learn a new skill. Kids will love spending time with you in the kitchen, both at this conservatory and at home.

How to be a best mom:

- Bake some cookies with your kids to deliver to the neighbors.
- Take some cooking classes yourself for a girls' night out.

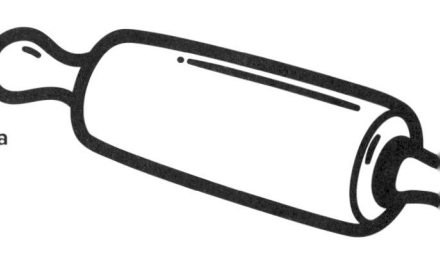

Best Mini Golf

MAGIC MINI GOLF

6160 Delmar Blvd. | 314-725-2222
magicminigolf.com

You'll have a magical time in the heart of the Delmar Loop! The animated sign, which won first place in an international sign competition, is neon and speaks to the electric atmosphere you will find inside. This mini golf destination is more than meets the 18-hole-course eye. The overall theme of the space is all things whimsy. In addition to the whimsically themed mini golf stops, there's a small Ferris wheel and even a wedding chapel where you wouldn't normally expect one to be. Much of the space is filled with nostalgic items that are both magic and golf themed from the personal collection of the mastermind behind this fun family-friendly attraction.

✓ How to be a best mom:

- **Play some pinball in the arcade.**
- **Challenge your kids to a game of shuffleboard.**

ALOHA MINI GOLF

13502 Big Bend Rd. | 314-330-4869
alohastl.com

You'll say mahalo for all-you-can-play mini golf!! For over 10 years this has been a preferred tropical destination in Valley Park. It's easy to feel like you are golfing in the islands as you go from hole to hole because you'll advance over water via bridges to the next challenge.

Instead of a windmill obstacle, the ball goes over the water by way of a trough that extends to the next island. This course isn't just about bragging rights; if you get a hole-in-one on the randomly assigned hole of the day, you'll win a free Hawaiian shave ice. Your family will love the outdoor setting that feels like a park with the many water features, real rock structures, and plants.

✓ How to be a best mom:

- If you don't win one, get a refreshing and delicious Hawaiian shave ice from the silver train caboose shack.
- Go in the evening or at night to enjoy playing under the tiki lights.

PUTTSHACK

3730 Foundry Way, Ste. 100 | 314-887-7888
puttshack.com

You'll have a high-tech par 3! This miniature golf venue is unlike any other and takes care of it all for you. Well, almost all. The only thing that's not done for you is your putt. Enter your name into the system and your golf ball is tracked with technology. The number of times it takes to reach the hole and your score are all recorded for you, making it the perfect place for families because you don't have to worry about messing with paper and pencils. An industrial setting with neon lights, decorative graffiti, and lively music add to the overall atmosphere that your family will enjoy.

✓ How to be a best mom:

- Register online so it's done before you get there.
- Grab a delectable treat from Patty's Cheesecake right there on-site in the Foundry.

Best Place to Learn to Play Golf

Courtesy of Barbara Northcott

TOWER TEE

6727 Heege Rd. | 314-833-3322
towertee.com

You'll enjoy the return of a St. Louis landmark! After being a popular golf course for over 50 years, the original Tower Tee closed in 2018. A more modernized complex of golf recreation has since made its return in the exact same spot, with the exact same name. Kids will enjoy learning to play the game with options like private lessons, day camps, and leagues. The new and improved golf and recreation center consists of a par 3 course and 9 holes on lush greens with traditional sand bunkers. It's the perfect setting for grabbing pictures of your kids practicing their new skills. There are even separate putting greens that pay homage to other local favorites like Cardinals baseball, Blues hockey, and the Saint Louis Zoo.

✓ How to be a best mom:

- Play a round on the footgolf course or bocce ball.
- Swing a bat instead of a club at the batting cages found right next to the playground.

Kids will enjoy learning to play the game.

FAMILY GOLF AND LEARNING CENTER

3717 Tree Court Industrial Blvd. | 636-861-2500
familygolfonline.com

You'll learn from the pros! More than a course, this golfing venue is an experience. In addition to camps, clinics, and leagues, this golf center offers both private and group lessons. The instructors who teach at Family Golf have extensive training and most have credentials with the Professional Golfers' Association. Individual and family memberships are available for a full year, six months, or three months with access to the lush and rolling green courses. This golf center is beautifully kept and set in nature, being just across the road from the Meramec River. Kids will feel like they are on tour with the PGA as they travel to different courses with the simulator game, and the entire family can learn together at this great training center.

✓ How to be a best mom:

- Rent the terrace, book tee times for all their friends, or party in one of the driving range bays for your little golfer's birthday.
- Drive into the main part of Kirkwood after a lesson and enjoy an ice cream treat at either Andy's Frozen Custard or Clementine's Naughty & Nice Creamery.

THE HIGHLANDS GOLF & TENNIS

5163 Clayton Ave. | 314-531-7773
highlandsgolfandtennis.com

You'll golf in the park! The course that's located in the end of Forest Park is very close to the hustle and bustle of a major medical center, but you'd never know it due to the serene setting. This is the place for kids to learn to golf all summer long with several summer camp packages to choose from. Everything is thought of and taken care of for you with the weekly rates, including lunch. There's also a before and after care option if that's something you need. Kids can, of course, learn to play the sport all year long with either private or group instruction, or by hitting the course with a family member who knows the game.

✓ How to be a best mom:

- After a golf lesson, head to The Cup in the Central West End for a cupcake treat.
- Try out learning to play tennis.

CRESTWOOD BOWL

9822 Watson Rd., Crestwood | 314-966-4377
crestwoodbowl.com

You'll learn to bowl on historic Route 66! Step inside this bowling alley that feels authentic to days gone by. This heart of the Crestwood community first opened in 1958, and it's one of the only bowling alleys in the area that teaches the sport through "learn to play." These special Saturday-morning leagues are designed to spark the interest of the younger generation. The Bumper Bowl League is for ages up to 6 years and will avoid the gutter entirely. There are two additional leagues for older children and teens. Lighter-weight bowling balls are always available as well as ramps to assist kids in guiding the ball down the center of the lane.

✓ How to be a best mom:

- Make sure to bring a pair of socks if your kids are wearing sandals on the day you go.
- Sign up for "kids bowl free this summer."

BOWLERO

1254 Dougherty Ferry Rd., Valley Park | 636-225-2400
176 Four Seasons Shop Center, Chesterfield | 314-469-6550
bowlero.com

You'll have a lively time unlike any other! From the tables with diner chairs to the classic bowling atmosphere, this entire space has a fun, retro feel. Whether it's a birthday party or just family fun, this bowling center has it all. The impressive size with 40 lanes and a state-of-the-art arcade, which includes several different types of claw machines, makes this venue much more than just a traditional bowling alley. Wittily named foods and drinks at the concessions counter will bring out all the smiles. There are also three locations to choose from in the St. Louis area.

✓ How to be a best mom:

- Bowling is the perfect day-off-from-school activity, particularly because lanes are often filled with leagues playing in the evenings during the school year.
- Check the bowling and food special pricing to better plan your visit.

OLIVETTE LANES

9520 Olive Blvd., Olivette | 314-991-0365
olivettelanes.com

You'll not just regular bowl, you'll Cosmic Bowl! This bowling alley starts Cosmic Bowling at 6 p.m. on Fridays so it's perfect for families to be able to enjoy. Kids will love participating in the Saturday-morning leagues designed just for them. The 10-week sessions run year-round and will create fun memories of learning a new skill. Neither Fridays nor Saturdays are dedicated to league play (except for Saturday morning for kids), so there are plenty of open lanes for the public. The fun music playing in this bowling alley will indeed have you dancing as you roll the ball down the lane.

✓ How to be a best mom:

- Go online to book a lane and you will also be able to see availability when leagues are happening during the week.
- Get a Dad's Famous Oatmeal Cookie from the on-site bar and grill.

Best Place to See Smaller Sports Teams

GATEWAY GRIZZLIES

2301 Grizzlie Bear Blvd., Sauget, IL | 618-337-3000
gatewaygrizzlies.com

You'll watch a game of the national pastime while being so close to the field! With just 6,000 seats in this stadium, there's no need for binoculars. Conveniently located just eight miles from downtown St. Louis, with free parking and low-cost ticket pricing, this ballpark is perfect for families. There's an entire kids zone with a full-size playground, outdoor games, and even a bounce house. All is included with your seat ticket and adds to the memories created while watching a quality baseball game. Your kids will get a kick out of "Baseball's Best Burger" that uses glazed donuts as the bun. Kids will also love trying to catch a foul ball or a home run that's hit out to the grassy hill. It's a family-friendly event you will want to attend again and again.

✓ How to be a best mom:

- Save big with a family four-pack of tickets that includes hot dogs, drinks, and chips.
- Bring a permanent marker or pen with you to get autographs after the game.

SAINT LOUIS BILLIKENS

Chaifetz Arena | 1 S Compton Ave.
slubillikens.com

You'll experience the luck of the Billiken! Just because there's no NBA team in St. Louis doesn't mean you can't enjoy a rousing game of b-ball. This college basketball team puts on a talented game, and the self-proclaimed World's Greatest Pep Band will have you dancing in your seats. The usual types of sporting event foods are available at concessions, and there's always a fun halftime show for the entire family to enjoy. If you aren't lucky enough to catch a shirt from the cheerleaders' air cannon, there are booths to find all the blue-and-white merch.

✓ How to be a best mom:

- Find the Billiken statue in front of the arena; have kids rub his belly and make a wish.
- Get season tickets so you never miss a game.

HIGH SCHOOL SPORTS

A high school near you.

You'll show support for your home team! When it comes to sporting events, high schools have it all. From baseball to basketball, hockey to lacrosse, football to wrestling, swimming to water polo, soccer to tennis and many others, just about every type of sport is represented in your own community. These teens work hard, have great talent, and love to hear fans cheering them on. Kids will enjoy attending and telling you about what activity they will participate in one day. There are multiple sports taking place during the school year so be sure to check the schedules and attend a few during the season.

✓ How to be a best mom:

- The school's marching band will have competitions that you can attend.
- Attend the homecoming game wearing the school colors.

Best Outdoor Place for Family Pictures

SHAW NATURE RESERVE

307 Pinetum Loop Rd., Gray Summit
314-577-9555
missouribotanicalgarden.org/plan-your-visit/family-of-attractions/shaw-nature-reserve

You'll find miles of picture-taking spots in Gray Summit! This 2,441-acre nature reserve is an extension of Missouri Botanical Garden and has so many areas perfect for capturing your family. The reserve's beautiful fall colors are known for providing a perfect backdrop for family pictures, and the atmosphere allows kids to feel more at ease with picture taking due to all the extra space. In spring and summertime there are ample amounts of wildflowers to add color in your photos. No matter the time of year, there are great options, because in winter the crisp mist rising from the lake and open fields will provide an enchanting setting. There are also several historic buildings that will add unique features in the background of your family pictures.

Courtesy of Catherine Donze

✓ How to be a best mom:

- Plan to spend some time in the sensory garden where kids can climb a smaller-scale fire tower, climb logs, swing, and experience nature in a whole new way.
- Go bird-watching on one of the many shorter hikes.

FAUST PARK

15025 Faust Park, Chesterfield | 314-615-8336
stlouiscountymo.gov/st-louis-county-departments/parks/places/faust-park

You'll step back in time as you take family pictures! Throughout this park setting you'll find historic buildings that were hand selected to be moved to the site. These structures create an old-fashioned village that's perfect for family pictures. Your photographer can snap away as you stroll along the paths, stand in the village gardens, and sit on any number of the many beautiful front porches from the past. Kids will particularly like standing in front of an old schoolhouse for a picture. There's even a rustic barn that serves as a great backdrop and plenty of trees that add a nature look to pictures.

✓ How to be a best mom:

- Get tickets to take a ride on the St. Louis Carousel or spend a couple of hours at the Sophia M. Sachs Butterfly House, both of which are on the park grounds.
- Plan on some extra time to visit the playground.

SANDY CREEK COVERED BRIDGE STATE HISTORIC SITE

9090 Old Lemay Ferry Rd., Hillsboro | 636-464-2976
mostateparks.com/park/sandy-creek-covered-bridge-state-historic-site

You'll have your family captured in front of a historic covered bridge! Built in 1872, this bridge is one of four remaining covered bridges in all of Missouri. This particular one actually has the perfect look for family pictures for holiday cards, especially if there's snow on the ground. The red wood Howe truss bridge is beautiful in any season but feels festive at the holidays. Kids will enjoy walking through it, and those pictures will undoubtedly turn out great. Even the wooden fencing lining the lane leading up to the covered bridge makes a pretty backdrop for photos.

✓ How to be a best mom:

- Be on the lookout for special events taking place at this site, like night stargazing.
- Print off the bird checklist to look for the 110 species of birds that have been recorded in the area.

Best Selfie and Instagram Photo Ops

ST. LOUIS GRAFFITI WALL

1000 S Wharf St.

You'll find new artistic backdrops for your selfies each year! For over 25 years, the floodwall along the Mississippi River has been showcasing the talent of artists nationwide. This wall has become a two-mile-long outdoor art gallery featuring graffiti of all skill levels. The colorful walls are perfect for taking photos in front of, and you can either drive, walk, or bike down the entire length. Kids (and the rest of the family) will be amazed by the talent on display and will have a difficult time deciding which part of the canvas to take a picture in front of.

✓ How to be a best mom:

- Attend the Paint Louis festival at the Graffiti Wall to see the new art going up.
- Have kids make their own graffiti wall at home using poster board.

COLUMBIA BOTTOM CONSERVATION AREA

801 Strodtman Rd. | 636-441-4554
mdc.mo.gov/discover-nature/places/columbia-bottom-conservation-area

You'll have nature photobomb your pic! There's not much that can be done with land that floods, but the Missouri Department of Conservation has created a field of dreams for photographers and Instagrammers alike. Field after field of bright yellow sunflowers appear in July and August. The flowers with a sunny disposition are the perfect backdrop for pictures of your kids. There are photo opportunities next to the flowers, in the flowers, and from the observation platforms. Use #ColumbiaBottomSunflowers on your social media posts to share your stunning pictures as you document summer life.

How to be a best mom:

- Hire a photographer to get some candid family shots in the field.
- Take bug spray and plan accordingly if the fields are muddy.

SELFIE WRLD

18521 Outlet Blvd., Ste. 704, Chesterfield | 636-778-0608
selfiewrldstl.com

You'll take creative pictures in the first selfie museum in St. Louis! More than just a unique space, there are 25 rooms within 1,800 square feet to take selfie after selfie. Each room has backdrops and ring lights so all you need is your phone camera to document the fun. Kids will love pretending with milkshakes, burgers, and fries props in the diner while you click-click away. Additional rooms feature props like real playground swings and a fun watermelon background. There's even an airplane room with a blue sky and clouds outside the windows for your little fan of flying. Lots of neon and color will really make your photos pop.

How to be a best mom:

- Let your kids pick out their own outfit changes or hats to bring from home.
- Bring your DSLR camera along for taking photos (there's no extra charge).

great idea!

Best Staycation

ST. LOUIS UNION STATION HOTEL

1820 Market St. | 314-231-1234
stlouisunionstation.com

You'll feel like you've left the area but are still in downtown! It's no secret that a historic train station sits in the heart of downtown. The majestic stone edifice and clock tower is easily spotted right on Market Street. First opening in 1894, it now houses a hotel and is the perfect destination for a local staycation. Everything needed to have a fun family vacation is all in one place! From various types of attractions to several on-site dining options, there's something for everyone to enjoy. The kids will like taking a dip in the outdoor pool as well as seeing the fountains in the enclosed area between the hotel and the St. Louis Aquarium.

✓ *How to be a best mom:*

- Take the kids to the free light shows in the Grand Hall and at the lake outside that run nightly.
- Don't forget swimming suits for the outdoor pool in summer.

Courtesy of Don Korte

PERE MARQUETTE LODGE

13653 Lodge Blvd., Grafton, IL | 618-786-2331
pmlodge.net

You'll marvel at the thick stone wall construction of this historic lodge! Explore the numerous hiking trails, go swimming in the indoor pool, read a book next to the massive fireplace while the kids are playing on the giant chess board, and take in all the views from up on a hill along the Mississippi River. The over-8,000-acre state park has so much to offer for a weekend away. There's even horseback riding nearby at Pere Marquette Riding Stables. This destination up the River Road just north of Grafton, Illinois, is a staycation you will want to do again and again.

✓ *How to be a best mom:*

- Go in January or February to look for the eagles that nest in the trees along the River Road.
- Take a puzzle or card game to enjoy as a family in the main lodge.

THE LANDING HUB

1 Landing Hub Ln., Pacific | 636-393-0778
landinghub.com

You'll vacation where it's more than just a location by a theme park! This staycation destination with a modern vibe has been open for over two years and it's the perfect place to stay near Six Flags—even more perfect due to the guest rooms that are large with families in mind. With guest quarters that have bunk beds in addition to regular beds and sofa sleepers, as well as kitchen and laundry space in the room, nothing has been forgotten when it comes to family travel. As the kids look around at the refreshing pool, 18-hole disc golf course, pickleball court, table tennis, pool table, and basketball hoop, they will undoubtably beg to skip a day at the amusement park to just spend time at this fabulous boutique resort. Fun for the entire family, there are also seven acres of wooded area to hike and explore outside.

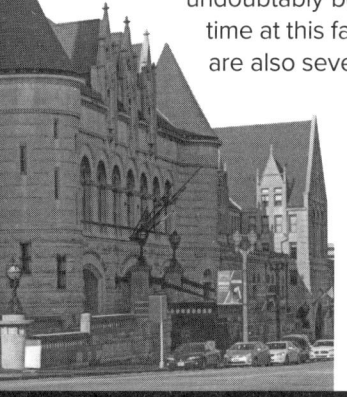

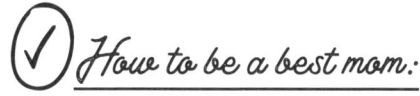

✓ *How to be a best mom:*

- Book a *Star Wars*–inspired room and stay together as a family in a specially designed sleeping pod.
- Borrow some board games from the common area and have a family game night.

Best Place for Your Car Enthusiast

NORTH CENTRAL HOBBIES

9630 Lackland Rd., Overland | 314-426-0031
nchobby.net

You'll cheer your car on while learning the curves of the track! At the only slot car racing track in the area that's open to the public, Friday nights at 7 p.m. are all about family time. Carrera Digital 132 slot cars hug the corners of this one-of-a-kind track. Every few months there's a new track configuration laid out on the elevated Astroturf, and kids will be amazed by the automatic lane switching with just the touch of a button. The regulars are enthusiasts themselves and happy to share their knowledge, especially with the younger generation of racers. This hobby shop also carries cars, tracks, parts, and more for taking the fun home.

✓ How to be a best mom:

- Customize your own car in hopes of setting a new track record.
- Plan ahead to go next door for a treat at Skeeters Frozen Custard before or after racing.

You'll cheer your car on while learning the curves of the track!

ST. LOUIS CAR MUSEUM & SALES

1575 Woodson Rd. | 314-993-1330 | stlouiscarmuseum.com

You'll enter a car lover's dream! The parking lot might appear to be empty but that's just due to its sheer size to have ample amounts of space for outdoor car shows. While some of the classic cars found inside are permanent fixtures of the museum, there are often vehicles coming and going through sales. Kids will enjoy going around with the sales sheet to see just how much these cars go for and will be amazed by the most expensive price on the list. Classic toys and classic pedal cars are also part of the self-guided tour. There's even a historic popcorn wagon that will have you craving the popped treat, so you might just have to drop by one of the many gourmet popcorn shops in St. Louis on your way home.

✓ How to be a best mom:

- Attend the car show that's held out front each year at back-to-school time.
- Pick out a song on the jukebox.

ST. LOUIS DIRT BURNERS R/C RACEWAY

2330 Marshall Rd., Kirkwood | 314-717-0260
dirtburners.org

You'll race cars in the dirt! With a setting along the Meramec River, it's no wonder that this R/C playground has been underwater more than a few times. This nonprofit club was originally formed by those with a passion for off-road R/C car racing, and they've created a truly remarkable place for hobbyists to enjoy. Every Saturday is racing day, and for a fee kids can jump into the race. Everyone is placed in a level at check-in that suits their abilities on the track. Those who join a race automatically become part of the club. There are events held throughout the year and bleachers to watch the races, so you don't always have to be a participant. The track is changed to create a new configuration two to three times a year. During the weekdays, the track is free and open to the public to enjoy so that's the perfect time to get out there and practice.

✓ How to be a best mom:

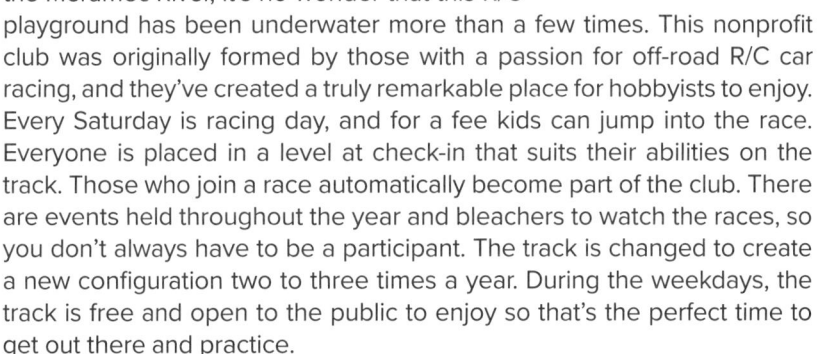

- Take along your bikes and take a family bike ride on the Meramec Greenway trail that runs right by the racing track.
- Go to Checkered Flag Hobby Country in South County to get car tips from an expert and purchase a car to race.

Best Place for the Train Enthusiast

THE NATIONAL MUSEUM OF TRANSPORTATION
2933 Barrett Station Rd. | 314-965-6212 | tnmot.org

You'll go back in time as you climb aboard antique train cars that once traveled east to west! Kids will love sitting in the engineer seat and pretending to feed coal into the engine. Be prepared to marvel at the enormous size of the Big Boy steam engine when standing in front of the locomotive. Admission includes a trolley ride, but you'll definitely want to add on the unlimited train rides and handcar rides. Kids with enthusiasm for locomotives will talk about that small-scale train adventure for weeks. The retired engineers are so friendly and informative. You can tell that they really enjoy seeing the kids' eyes light up when the train whistle blows.

How to be a best mom:

- Get a membership so you can return as often as you'd like.
- Add a Creation Station pass to your ticket for the little ones or book a birthday party in the transportation-themed play area.

WABASH FRISCO & PACIFIC RAILROAD

101 Grand Ave., Wildwood | 636-587-3538
wfprr.com

You'll find yourself calling out "All aboard!" as you walk toward these miniature steam engines! The entire concept of this railway in the woods began when railroad enthusiasts wanted to take their zeal into adulthood. While it originally started out near the airport, the historic community of Glencoe is now the perfect location for this charming railroad. Kids and adults alike will enjoy riding through nature in colorful open-air train cars that are, of course, small scale. The two-mile-long trip can afford opportunities to see wildlife or just meander along the scenic byways; either is enjoyable on this unconventional train ride.

How to be a best mom:

- Drop by Bluff View Park (located at 1900 Old State Rd. in Glencoe) and view the little trains going by down below.
- Don't miss the playground just down the lane from the tracks.

FRISCO TRAIN & TOY STORE

24 Front St., Valley Park | 636-529-1660
friscotrainstore.com

You'll want to yell "choo choo!" as you walk through the front door! Originally built as a hotel for railroad workers in the late 1800s, the building has been home to many different types of businesses over the years. Perhaps the favorite is what it is today, a train store that is steps away from an active train track. Your little train enthusiast will love to experience the huge, multilevel train table that takes up much of the front room. The main floor play area is open to the public, but donations are appreciated. There's an ample amount of seating around the room for observing while your child plays as well as an extensive line of wooden trains for sale around the shop.

How to be a best mom:

- Book a birthday party on the main floor or in the upper floor play areas.
- Look for the historic red caboose just across the train tracks outside.

COOL!

Best Place to Take a Plane Enthusiast

SMARTT FIELD AIRPORT OPEN HOUSE

6390 Grafton Ferry Rd., Portage Des Sioux | 636-949-7535
sccmo.org/237/Regional-Airport---Smartt-Field

You'll see pumpkins fall from the sky! The St. Charles County Regional Airport–Smartt Field sits on land between the Mississippi and Missouri Rivers. Each year nearing the end of October there's a special open house event at this airfield and it's one that families do not want to miss. Kids will be in awe as they watch World War II B-25 and TBM bombers soar through the air and then drop pumpkins onto targets below. There are additional family-friendly activities to enjoy at this event as well. Other times of the year this is a great area to park on the side of the road and see if you can spy smaller planes taking off or landing.

✓ How to be a best mom:

- Go bird-watching at the nearby Marais Temps Clair Conservation Area.
- Visit the historical landmark Our Lady of the Rivers Shrine, also in Portage Des Sioux.

BUDER PARK FLYING FIELD

400 Valley Park Rd., Valley Park
stlouisaeropilots.org

You'll find quite the bit of aeronautical history at this St. Louis County park! What started out as donated land next to the Meramec River in the late 1950s quickly morphed into a flying field for radio-controlled model planes. For over 60 years people have been building models of their own small-scale planes to fly at the Valley Park field. Permits are required to fly both model planes and drones at this park, and there's an entire flying club of R/C Aeropilots that you can join. Kids will enjoy watching the little aircraft being flown, seeing the orange wind sock blowing in the breeze, and attending the model airplane air shows throughout the year.

✓ How to be a best mom:

- Build a model plane with your kids.
- Take a hike on the Meramec Trail.

HISTORIC AIRCRAFT RESTORATION MUSEUM

3127 Creve Coeur Mill Rd., Maryland Heights
314-434-3368
historicaircraftrestorationmuseum.org

You'll walk through actual airplane hangars at Creve Coeur Airport! What started out as a place to store a private collection of airplanes is available for all to enjoy. Fabric-covered biplanes, World War II warcraft, and so many other historic planes in all sorts of colors can be found in the four different hangars of this museum. There's even one of the largest biplanes ever made. Some of the airplanes have been known to leave the hangar for testing out to see if they can still fly, but for the most part these planes are just to look at these days. A couple of the planes in the museum have even been stars of Hollywood in movies and television shows. With an active airfield just steps away, this is the perfect place to ignite a new generation of aviators.

✓ How to be a best mom:

- Watch for the Youth Aviation Day event that's put on by the Gateway Youth Aeronautical Foundation and held at Creve Coeur Airport.
- Go to your local library and check out some books on the planes you saw.

Best Place for Kids Who Love Science

SAINT LOUIS SCIENCE CENTER

5050 Oakland Ave. | 314-289-4400
slsc.org

You'll get up close to all things science, which includes a hungry Tyrannosaurus rex! This impressive science center has floor after floor of all the best hands-on exhibits. Kids who find the animatronic T. rex to be just a tad bit scary will still love learning about dinosaurs while digging for pretend fossils. The giant marble run contraption is neat to see in action as balls make loops through the intricate track, and it's in the perfect location to watch as you eat a snack at concessions. While the science center itself is free, there are ticketed attractions and events to enjoy separately. There are also various membership levels that come with extra perks like free parking, tickets to the OMNIMAX Theater and the McDonnell Planetarium, Discovery Room tickets, and more to add to the overall experience.

✓ How to be a best mom:

- Get tickets to see an educational program or popular movie on the IMAX Dome.
- Build an arch out of large, padded blocks with your kids or take a run on the human hamster wheel.

HEALTHWORKS! KIDS' MUSEUM ST. LOUIS

1100 Macklind Ave. | 314-241-7391
hwstl.org

You'll learn about health and have fun while doing it! What began in 1977 as the Delta Dental Health Theatre at Laclede's Landing in downtown St. Louis was reinvented and moved to its current location in 2004. While this museum is a popular educational destination for field trips, you don't have to be with a school to visit. Kids can experience health-learning theater shows and pretend to work in a dental office, medical office, pharmacy, or farmers market. There's even an enormous skeletal structure for kids to play on, complete with a slide going down the leg bone. Special events throughout the year and/or summer camp are sure to be a favorite for your kid who is all about fun, science, and health.

How to be a best mom:

- Host a birthday celebration in a party room that allows you to bring in your own food and drink.
- Get a yearly membership.

MAD SCIENCE

8420 Olive Blvd., Ste. R | 314-991-8000
stlouis.madscience.org

You'll have fun with science! Through after-school programs and camps, this organization brings science to life for kids who are elementary school ages. Hands-on and fun, kids are sure to enjoy making experiments that fizz and bubble. Kids will also learn about educational topics related to chemistry, biology, engineering, and physics—all at their level, of course. These specially designed classes are offered at many locations throughout the St. Louis area with some probably being in your own school district. Think of it as traveling science and an experience that kids will love being part of.

How to be a best mom:

- Have even more fun with science by bringing the activity to your own home in the form of a birthday party done by Mad Science.
- Get a microscope for your kids to continue the science fun at home.

Best Ice-Skating Rinks

STEINBERG SKATING RINK

400 Jefferson Dr. | 314-998-4582
steinbergrink.com

You'll skate on the largest outdoor ice rink in all of the Midwest! Just steps away from one of the many water areas of Forest Park is this popular ice-skating rink. Options are available for lessons, and the indoor/outdoor café is a favorite of many for delicious eats. Skating at night lets you enjoy the rink under the stars with the ambiance of the white string lights decorating the area. There are glowing firepits to warm yourself by, plenty of sessions to choose from, and lessons for all levels at this St. Louis winter tradition. In summer months the ice is replaced with a concrete rink for roller-skating, so it's truly a place that the family can enjoy all year long.

✓ How to be a best mom:

- Try out bumper cars on ice.
- Hit up any number of the fun events or festivals held at the rink, particularly in the spring and summer.

Courtesy of Ngoc Nguyen

WEBSTER GROVES ICE ARENA

33 E Glendale Rd., Webster Groves | 314-963-5621
webstergrovesmo.gov/197/Ice-Arena

You'll see a mix of skating styles on this full-size ice rink! Home to Webster Groves High School Skatesmen Hockey Club and Metro Edge Figure Skating Club, it's common for all levels of talented skaters to be on the ice. Depending on the schedule, there are public skating sessions, lessons, and cosmic skating. The rink offers different types of passes like per-session and individual season passes with discounts for more than one family member. So much more than just a sheet of ice with birthday party packages and rentable plastic seal-shaped ice-skating aids to help support those learning how to balance, this rink is fun for the entire family.

✓ How to be a best mom:

- Take your kids to see area skaters perform in *Nutcracker on Ice* or cheer from the stands when attending a high school hockey game.
- Don't forget to dress warm and take a pair of gloves.

THE LOADING DOCK ICE RINK

401 E Front St., Grafton, IL | 618-556-7951
graftonloadingdock.com

You'll skate at a popular on-the-river bar and grill location! While only open in the winter months, a smaller sheet of ice than most, and on the other side of the river, this rink is definitely worth checking out. Housed in an old warehouse connected to the Loading Dock restaurant, the rink's enchanting setup has firepits for making s'mores and strands of white lights draped across the ceiling. There are also quite a few festive, winter-themed backdrops that are perfect for snapping some pictures to use for the holiday card. Making this ice-skating destination a family tradition is always a good idea and one that the kids will talk about all year long.

✓ How to be a best mom:

- Escape the cold with a heated tent rental.
- Look for eagles as you drive up the river road.

Best Place to Spin Your Wheels

KINETIC PARK

7801 Town Square Ave., Dardenne Prairie | 636-278-1248
sccmo.org/741/Kinetic-Park

You'll be amazed by the largest outdoor skate park in all of Missouri! Grab your scooters, bikes, skateboards, or inline skates to experience 33,000 square feet of concrete adventure. This skate park is free, open to the public year-round, and filled with various levels of courses. Think deep bowls resembling in-ground pools (not filled with water, of course) that have ramps and hills scattered throughout—that's what you will find at this popular riding destination. There's a circuit course and specially designed side ramps just for bikes. A concession stand and picnic tables round out this skate park that your kids will ask to go to again and again.

✓ *How to be a best mom:*

- Check the schedule and attend one of the skate nights under the lights.
- Go visit the indoor climbing space, pickleball courts, and e-sports lounge that's also part of this park.

The largest outdoor skate park in all of Missouri!

RAMP RIDERS

2324 Salena St. | 314-776-4025
rampriders.net

You'll never be able to count how many half-pipes there are in this 30,000-square-foot rider's paradise! Open since 2000, an extensive number of skate and bike ramps fill the space. Tucked away inside an old warehouse, the vibe is industrial urban complete with graffiti-painted walls and glass skylights. There's a ramp for every age and level, with dedicated time on Sundays for kids and beginners. The special family time allows for caregivers to join the kids at no charge. Kids will love looking at the colorful roller skate wheels, BMX bikes, and board designs for sale in the skate shop.

✓ How to be a best mom:

- Sign kids up for private lessons to learn some moves and tricks on the scooter, bike, skateboard, or roller skates.
- Get a punch card for multiple return visits.

ST. LOUIS BMX BIKE PARK

4047 Mount Olive St., Lemay

You'll love the natural feel of this bike park! This destination for BMXers is located just off Grant's Trail in Lemay. Also known as the Figure 8 BMX Park, your kids will love testing out the park's dirt ramps. Whether or not they are proficient with the major ups and downs of the more advanced ramps, there are areas just the right size for beginners. The space consists of 28 acres dedicated to adventuring on a bike. More ramps and trails are continuously being constructed, so think of it as a changing landscape. This volunteer-run park is the place to spin your wheels or leave the ground. The park can be a bit tricky to find, so from the parking lot at the Mysun Charitable Foundation Trailhead of Grant's Trail, bike up the path that leads over the wooden bridge. Then about a quarter of a mile up and on your left you will find this unique biking playground.

✓ How to be a best mom:

- Don't forget to take along helmets and pads.
- Stop off at the small playground near the parking lot for added fun.

Best Swimming Pool

WAPELHORST AQUATIC FACILITY

1875 Muegge Rd., St. Charles | 636-949-3372
stcharlesparks.com/wapelhorst-aquatic-facility

You'll fly high on more than one waterslide! It's not often you find a public pool with even one waterslide, but this aquatic center has four different waterslides of varying intensities. The most adventurous will enjoy having their raft pushed up quickly by water before it comes flinging back down the slide on the Boomerang. This water park has a massive lazy river that meanders around with several inlets where you can stop and enjoy sitting in the cool water. The younger kids will love the area that's just their size with pop jets, a water play structure, and even their own smaller slides. There's ample seating in the shade at this aquatic center that's designed particularly with families in mind.

✓ *How to be a best mom:*

- Explore one of the fun park playgrounds before or after going to the pool.
- Take along a volleyball to play on one of the sand courts.

You'll fly high on more than one waterslide!

AQUAPORT

2344 McKelvey Rd., Maryland Heights
314-738-2599
marylandheights.com/visitors/aquaport

You'll be able to surf without going to the ocean! This aquatics center is popular for the FlowRider attraction that gives you the ability to surf and bodyboard (there are height requirements), but it's also more than just the best place to catch a wave in the area. There's a tube ride waterslide, a racing slide, and an enclosed tube slide that will spin riders into a bowl before dropping them into the pool below. In addition to the four water slides, there's a massive pool with a long lazy river going around it. The littlest kids of the family will particularly enjoy spending time in the shallow pool area with accompanying water-spraying features.

✓ How to be a best mom:

- Sign up for FlowRider lessons to learn how to catch a wave.
- Visit the playground just next door to Aquaport.

THE LODGE DES PERES

1050 Des Peres Rd., Des Peres | 314-835-6150
desperesmo.org/144/Aquatics

You'll swim indoors and outdoors! This pool is a favorite due to the amount of aquatic fun offered here. Multiple slides, at varying degrees of thrill, can be found in different locations of this aquatic center. There's even an enclosed tube slide that starts inside and wraps around the outside of the building before coming back in to splash down into the indoor pool. Outside there's a zero-entry pool and a lazy river to float on. The indoor pool has a wave pool that is set on a schedule. You will find a menu of delicious eats available at the concession stand, and there are ample tables for dining. This destination pool is one the entire family will enjoy.

✓ How to be a best mom:

- Sign up for swimming lessons or tot time.
- Book a swim party package for your little fish's birthday.

Best Place for Thrill Seekers

SLICK CITY ACTION PARK

17379 Edison Ave., Chesterfield
636-229-9899
slickcity.com/stlouiswest

You'll fly off a slide! This action park is all about bringing a favorite piece of playground equipment indoors. Put on a pair of CitySocks, grab a mat, and slide away. Everywhere you turn there's a thrilling slide to enjoy, and each one is its own vibrant color. Kids will enjoy racing each other headfirst down steep slides, flying off the end into a giant pillow, and twisting through corkscrews. There are even areas for kids who aren't as daring to have a good time, with swings and air courts. Kids under 45 inches in height can climb in the multilevel playland with slides that are just their size, so there's something for everyone in the family to enjoy.

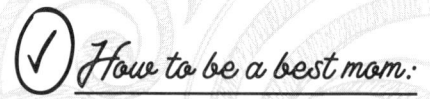

✓ How to be a best mom:

- Look for special promotions to maximize your fun and number of visits.
- Book a party just for fun, even when you're not celebrating a birthday.

SIX FLAGS

4900 Six Flags Rd., Eureka | 636-938-5300
sixflags.com/stlouis

You'll find thrill rides for the entire family to enjoy! With more than 45 rides and attractions, there's truly something for everyone. These days this amusement park is primarily Looney Tunes and DC Comics in theme, but it still has some of the original appeal of its early 1970s opening with charming areas like the Wild West and 1904 World's Fair sections. The littlest kids will enjoy the giant playscape and rides designed just for them in Bugs Bunny National Park. More daring, older children will gravitate to the roller coasters that go forward, backward, upside down, and everything in between. Cool off in the Hurricane Harbor water park where more thrills await.

✓ How to be a best mom:

- Leave a cooler with drinks and snacks in your car so kids can enjoy a refreshment on the way home after a long day at the theme park.
- Book a VIP Tour to celebrate a special day, or return again in the fall for Halloween fun.

AERIE'S ALPINE COASTER

600 Timber Ridge Dr., Grafton, IL | 618-786-8439
aeriesresort.com/coaster

You'll coast at speeds of up to 25 miles per hour down a bluff high above the Mississippi River! The first alpine coaster in Illinois is less than an hour away from St. Louis and worth the trip for the fun thrill. This self-controlled coaster uses gravity to propel riders down a metal rail track. To access the exciting ride, visitors must first take either a gondola or chairlift to the top. The view cannot be beat and only adds to the experience. This attraction is open year-round, allowing you to coast twists and turns over the snow. Kids will squeal in delight as they bank around each rounded corner. Nighttime rides with the track aglow are also an option, so be sure to add that to your bucket list.

✓ How to be a best mom:

- As you drive up the River Road, stop off to see the Piasa Bird.
- Get some tasty fudge on Main Street.

Best Freebie

VAT19

11783 Borman Dr.
vat19.com/tour

You'll see how a successful YouTube channel is made! If you have a YouTube fan in your house, then this is the free place you want to visit. Vat19 is a channel and website for purchasing merchandise that was first formed in 2000. Over the years it has achieved quite the bit of fame with receiving the Gold Play Button award for hitting one million subscribers and is on the fast track to receive the Diamond Play Button as they are nearing 10 million subscribers. Kids will love touring the soundstage, meeting the cast, and spinning the wheel at the end of the tour to win a prize. Shopping in the warehouse is always a favorite, as is the potential to be filmed for Vat19's social media. This is a great activity for a day off from school.

✓ How to be a best mom:

- Plan ahead by perusing vat19.com to pick out items for kids to purchase from the on-site warehouse, as the prices will be most accurate online.
- You can always shop locally without going on a tour; just enter at the Vat19 warehouse door.

GRANT'S FARM

7385 Grant Rd. | 314-843-1700 | grantsfarm.com

You'll see animals like bison, antelope, and deer roaming around as you weave through the Deer Park in an open-air tram! Free and open to the public (just pay for parking), this animal park has been a family favorite since it opened in 1954, but it was part of St. Louis history long before that. Originally the private residence for the Busch family (of the Anheuser-Busch Brewing Company), the 281-acre property located just outside of the city has become both a landmark and a tradition. Kids will love feeding the goats, seeing the various animals in their own habitats, and watching the fun animal shows.

✓ How to be a best mom:

- Register to take a private tour or plan to attend one of the many events throughout the year including Halloween Nights and the drive-through light display at Christmastime.
- Purchase a value fun pass that includes a snow cone, a ticket to ride the carousel, and bottles of milk to feed the goats.

CHOCOLATE CHOCOLATE CHOCOLATE COMPANY

5025 Pattison Ave. | 314-338-3501
chocolatechocolate.com

You'll satisfy your sweet tooth in more ways than one by learning how chocolate confections are made! Factory tours are free with reservations five days a week. Everyone taking a tour is required to wear a paper hat decorated with the Chocolate Chocolate Chocolate logo, and kids will love taking the souvenir home. The hats are also perfect for pictures at the factory to remember the experience. Getting a sample to taste is also part of seeing how the chocolates are made. For over two generations this chocolate business has been a favorite for families. The name itself was for the founder's three children, so family is very important here.

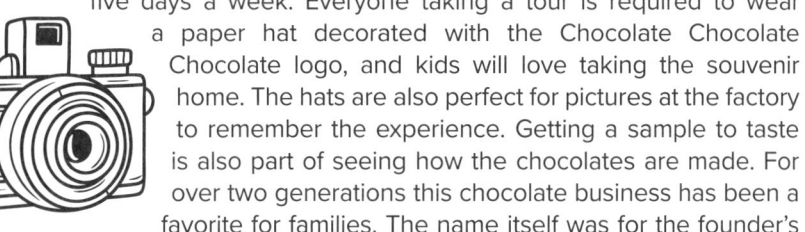

✓ How to be a best mom:

- If you don't have time for a tour then visit one of the other locations throughout the area to purchase quality chocolate.
- Ask about the oops bags of chocolates priced at a deal.

Best Place to Have a Birthday Party

AMP UP

13901 Manchester Rd., Town and Country | 314-439-8008
ampupactionpark.com

You'll have a really amped-up birthday! This action park has everything from a ropes course stretching high above the arcade to virtual reality and go-kart racing. There's something for all levels and ages to enjoy, with older kids (14 and up) being able to try their hand at axe throwing. For many kids, the ultimate action-packed favorite is laser tag. Black lights, colorful neon glowing decor, and loud music fill the exclusive arena, making it an immersive good time. There are various types of birthday packages to choose from, each coming with pizza, drinks, and even the paper plates. Kids are sure to have a lively and dynamic time.

✓ How to be a best mom:

- Bring along your own cake or cupcakes.
- Make team T-shirts for laser tag.

SWING-A-ROUND FUN TOWN

335 Skinker Ln., Fenton | 636-349-7077
sarfuntown.com

You'll have a party like you remember from your own childhood! Everything about this amusement venue is nostalgic, from the arcade center to the classic bumper boats. Most all of the attractions are included in the birthday party packages, making it an across-the-board fun time. Everyone will enjoy the outdoor mini golf with its colorful onion dome castle, intricate putting greens, and water features. In addition to the great birthday packages, the birthday kid gets to spin a prize wheel. Don't miss out on the indoor bumper cars and outdoor go-kart racing. No matter the weather, there's a party to be had either indoors or out.

✓ *How to be a best mom:*

- Take your school-age kids' report cards in to be rewarded with arcade play for all their As and Bs.
- Add on some arcade cards to the birthday party package.

BUILD-A-BEAR ADVENTURE

17353 Edison Ave., Chesterfield | 636-237-6101
buildabear.com/adventure-store

You'll walk into a Build-A-Bear Workshop and have a magical party! The first of its kind for the Build-A-Bear brand, this ultimate party place is where birthday dreams come true. Various party packages are available to choose from, with creative add-ons like face painting and having a visit from the Build-A-Bear mascot. Every package comes with a furry friend, access to an arcade that's just the right size, and a party room to help create a memorable time. There are even adorable selfie stations for kids to take pictures with their furry and nonfurry friends. So much more is on the horizon with this new concept party destination, so keep it in mind for school events and troop parties in addition to birthdays.

✓ *How to be a best mom:*

- Go to this location to create and adopt a furry friend.
- Make a reservation to decorate cupcakes in the Bakeshop.

Best At-Home Birthday Party Add-On

PREMIER ENTERTAINMENT

636-734-2083
bookmagicnow.com

You'll have a birthday at home that's filled with all the party activities! The connoisseur of parties knows what kids like when it comes to fun. Brian Styles is the St. Louis Balloon Guy, and he's an artist who doesn't just twist balloons into animals. While making all sorts of balloon creations magically right before your eyes, he also tells jokes and interacts with the party guests. Speaking of magic, this entertainment profession also has options for magic shows. Face painting and caricature art is yet another popular station to have at the birthday party that has everything.

✓ How to be a best mom:

- Book a foam party for outside fun, or order some balloon decor for your party theme.
- Get the neighbors together to have a block party that the kids will not forget.

DANDY SOFT SERVE

314-603-1515
dandysoftserve.com

You'll scream for ice cream! The delicacy that is an ice-cream cone was first introduced in Forest Park at the 1904 World's Fair, so having ice cream at a St. Louis birthday party is always a fun addition. This local business rents stainless steel industrial soft-serve ice cream machines that are the real deal. They also carry various flavors of ice cream mix from vanilla to chocolate to the popular Dole pineapple soft-serve that will have you thinking of your favorite theme park. One bag of mix yields approximately 80 to 90 servings, so it's great for all sizes of parties. Kids will love stepping up to the machine, pulling down the lever, and watching in wonder as their eyes tell them to take a serving bigger than their stomach.

✓ *How to be a best mom:*

- Get a keg of root beer from Fitz's to make refreshing floats with vanilla soft-serve ice cream.
- Make a toppings table with different candies, sprinkles, syrups, sugar cones, etc.

COWBOY CRITTERS

636-306-2500
cowboycritters.com

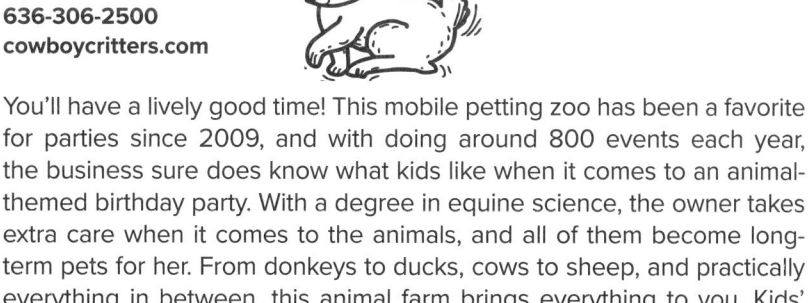

You'll have a lively good time! This mobile petting zoo has been a favorite for parties since 2009, and with doing around 800 events each year, the business sure does know what kids like when it comes to an animal-themed birthday party. With a degree in equine science, the owner takes extra care when it comes to the animals, and all of them become long-term pets for her. From donkeys to ducks, cows to sheep, and practically everything in between, this animal farm brings everything to you. Kids' favorites are feeding the goats, petting the soft rabbits, and observing the turtles. There are pigs available to book, but don't be surprised if they aren't as interactive or cuddly as other animals. This type of party is not just fun, it's an entire theme.

✓ *How to be a best mom:*

- For equestrian fans, request pony rides to be at your party.
- Book a pony dressed up as a unicorn with custom-color hair.

Best Place to See Santa

PLAZA FRONTENAC

1701 S Lindbergh Blvd. | 314-432-6760
plazafrontenac.com

You'll meet the fanciest Santa! Located in the South Court of Plaza Frontenac, this jolly man in red has long been known as the best mall Santa in the area. Pretty holiday decorations add to the experience with photo-taking options available. The magic of Christmas is everywhere you look. Reservations are encouraged to shorten your wait time, and there are quite a few different photo packages to choose from. Kids will wait all year just to tell this visitor from the North Pole what they'd like to find under the tree on Christmas morning.

This jolly man in red has long been known as the best mall Santa!

✓ *How to be a best mom:*

- Stop by one of the many local eateries either before or after your visit with Santa.
- Pick out a piece of handcrafted chocolate at Bissinger's in the mall.

THE POLAR EXPRESS TRAIN RIDE

201 S 18th St. | 314-942-6942
stlpolarexpressride.com

You'll take a train ride with the big man in red! An entertaining and out-of-the-ordinary way to meet Santa, this train to the North Pole departs Union Station and features the beloved storybook being recited along the way. Whimsical characters from the book interact with passengers as they dance in the aisles. Everyone gets a large chocolate chip cookie placed at their seat, and hot chocolate arrives as you journey. This holiday experience is fun for the entire family, and kids will love receiving their very own silver bell from Santa himself. Only those who believe will hear the bell ring, and it's a cute addition for your Christmas tree.

✓ How to be a best mom:

- Take lots of pictures with the festive backdrops in the activity tent before you board the train.
- Plan to return to Union Station on another day to have pancakes with Santa for breakfast in the Grand Hall.

BRUNCH WITH SANTA

601 Clark Ave. | 314-345-9880
mlb.com/cardinals/cardinals-nation

You'll participate in a favored St. Louis pastime with the man from the North Pole! Baseball and brunch are combined with time spent with Santa. Don't forget Fredbird; he will be there too. In addition to a delicious breakfast, there are many festive activities for the kids to enjoy at this holiday event. The type of activity may vary, but it's most likely face painting, balloon animals, writing letters to Santa, or something of the like. Kids will love getting pictures taken with both Santa and Fredbird. This event also includes admission to the Cardinals Museum, making this a definite holiday favorite for baseball fans.

✓ How to be a best mom:

- After things have settled down from the busy holidays, go back to Cardinal Nation in the new year for Family Night with Fredbird.
- Plan to arrive early so you have extra time to park at Ballpark Village, and check to see if validation is available for free parking.

Best Holiday Lights

GARDEN GLOW

4344 Shaw Blvd. | 314-577-5100
missouribotanicalgarden.org

You'll wander the Missouri Botanical Garden at night and be in wonder of the spectacular display! Whether or not there is snow on the ground, more than one million lights create a winter wonderland. Even the historic buildings of the garden get in on the action with holiday decor. There are many different photo opportunities, like giant picture frames that are in front of festive sitting areas and an oversize snow globe that kids will love climbing into. Sure to become a family-favorite holiday tradition each year, this winter activity is perfect for creating glowing memories.

How to be a best mom:

- Get some hot chocolate and s'mores from a refreshment stand.
- Take your kids to walk through the garden maze.

WINTER WONDERLAND

9551 Litzsinger Rd. | 314-615-4386
winterwonderlandstl.com

You'll see Tilles Park in a whole new light! For over 35 years, this holiday light display has been a well-known community favorite. In years past, there were a few different ways to experience the splendor. Perhaps taking Santa's sleigh, a carriage ride, or even walking through the lights will again make their appearance, but for now tickets are for drive-through viewing. Everyone will enjoy hearing festive tunes along the way and be in awe of the synchronized lights that give the illusion of flowing water. Fun decorative displays like the 12 Days of Christmas and a wall made from strands of lights add to the dazzling atmosphere. No matter the way you see the lights, this multigenerational favorite is one that's sure to continue on forever.

✓ How to be a best mom:

- Bring a thermos of hot chocolate to both enjoy and add warmth on a cold evening.
- Get a few families together and commission a limousine to travel through the lights.

HOLIDAY LIGHTS AT GRANT'S FARM

7385 Grant Rd. | 314-843-1700
grantsfarm.com

You'll see the Busch family estate like you never have before! While this light display is relatively on the newer side, it has quickly become one that is the talk of the town. There are options to drive through or walk through, and you may just want to try out both. Each gives a different feel to the festive season. The carousel looks even more magical at night with the additional glow from the holiday displays, and the biergarten draws everyone in with the enchanting courtyard. The entire family will love going through the tunnel of lights and seeing the massive size of the mansion up close.

✓ How to be a best mom:

- Get tickets to have breakfast with Santa, or reserve a firepit next to Mirror Lake.
- Continue the holiday season with the Busch family by going to the brewery lights in the city.

Best Festival

THE GREAT FOREST PARK BALLOON RACE

Forest Park Central Fields
greatforestparkballoonrace.com

You'll get as close as you can to hot-air balloons without leaving the ground! For over 50 years the Great Forest Park Balloon Race has encouraged glances upward in anticipation of seeing even just one hot-air balloon racing across the St. Louis sky. Generations have also enjoyed the evening before when the balloons are parked in the Central Fields area of Forest Park. Kids will love walking among the inflated balloons and asking the aeronauts questions at the Balloon Glow. Some of these specialty pilots even give out a trading card about their balloon. Every few minutes a horn will sound, signaling the balloons to be lit. It's an awesome display of dozens of balloons illuminating the night sky at one time. You'll also find sponsors and vendor booths with fun photo opportunities and giveaways in addition to other activities, food trucks, concessions, and live music.

✓ How to be a best mom:

- Visit on the day of the race to experience Purina sponsoring an entire area that's geared toward kids with inflatables and games.
- Stock up on glow sticks before heading down to the park.

STRAWBERRY FESTIVAL

Downtown Kimmswick | 636-464-7407
gokimmswick.com

You'll celebrate the sweet tastes of strawberry season the first weekend in June! Food and craft vendors abound at this two-day event. Just over 30 minutes from St. Louis, it's a festival very much worth traveling to. While it isn't the largest festival that the community of Kimmswick hosts (that happens in the fall), it's a great way to kick off the start of summer fun. The name of the celebration speaks for itself; everything is about the delicious red berries, but there's so much more to this festival than treats like strawberry shortcake, chocolate-covered strawberries, and strawberry cheesecake. Kids in particular will love the petting zoo, pony rides, bounce houses, and popular festival foods like funnel cakes, kettle corn, hamburgers, and hot dogs.

✓ How to be a best mom:

- Buy some fresh strawberries at the festival to make some jam at home with your kids.
- Return to Kimmswick in the fall for the Apple Butter Festival.

FESTIVAL OF NATIONS

Tower Grove Park, Main Dr. | 314-330-3587
festivalofnationsstl.org

You'll tour more than 75 nations in Tower Grove! This is a great educational opportunity for kids to learn about other cultures, from their food and traditions to art and music. For two whole days the community comes together to share different cultural backgrounds. What makes each nation distinct is experienced, celebrated, and embraced. The event is one that will captivate a variety of ages and open new windows of understanding. There are plenty of vendor booths to find one-of-a-kind wares that will be fun to incorporate into your own home. The entire family can also enjoy unfamiliar cuisine. It's a great way to teach kids that as much as we are different, we have many similarities.

✓ How to be a best mom:

- Go on a scavenger hunt to find specific flags of countries represented at the festival.
- Take your kids to cool off by wading in the park's Muckerman Fountain and playing in the water pop jets.

Best Membership

THE MAGIC HOUSE

516 S Kirkwood Rd. | 314-822-8900
magichouse.org

You'll think of your own childhood around every corner in this children's museum! Adults who grew up in 1980s St. Louis have fond memories visiting the newly (at the time) opened children's museum in the heart of Kirkwood. These days they enjoy taking their own crew to experience the nostalgic static ball and three-story slide that is still very much a part of the Victorian mansion. With the Family Plus Membership (that includes entry for the Magic House MADE for Kids) to a membership that includes grandparents or other caregivers, there's a membership level to fit every type of family. Kids (particularly those under 10) will love visiting the various attractions and exhibits throughout the year, climbing the giant beanstalk, exploring magical areas dedicated to education, and pretend play in the child-size village.

✓ *How to be a best mom:*

- Make your child's birthday even more magical with a themed party at the Magic House!
- Get a photo button made with the static ball.

You'll think of your own childhood around every corner in this children's museum!

MISSOURI BOTANICAL GARDEN

4344 Shaw Blvd. | 314-577-5100
missouribotanicalgarden.org

You'll get a membership that is three in one! Originally known as Shaw's Garden, this space was opened to the public in 1859 when Henry Shaw graciously shared his garden. It's now 79 acres of beautiful oasis surrounded by city. All membership levels include admission to the Missouri Botanical Garden, Sophia M. Sachs Butterfly House, and Shaw Nature Reserve. The Friends and Family membership level is a favorite due to the free tram tours and free admission to the Children's Garden while both are in season.

✓ How to be a best mom:

- Kids will love exploring the children's area beneath the Climatron and the two hedge mazes on the garden's grounds.
- For an added adventure, be sure to have quarters on hand to purchase food to feed the koi fish in the lake, or sign up for fun summer camps.

ST. LOUIS AQUARIUM AT UNION STATION

201 S 18th St. | 314-923-3900
stlouisaquarium.com

You'll board a pretend train that goes under the ocean! Annual pass holders can return again and again throughout the year by simply reserving an entry time. This fun aquarium is broken up into areas that represent the various aquatic regions of Missouri, allowing you to then travel upward to ocean life. Home to the world-famous blue lobster named Lord Stanley, playful river otters, and eerie Shark Canyon, there's something for everyone in the family to find interesting. Kids will love the touch pools for petting sharks, translucent jellyfish, and starfish. There's even a specially designed area with fun play tunnels for toddlers to get their wiggles out. This destination is sure to become a favorite for aquatic adventures.

✓ How to be a best mom:

- Print off #flatlordstanley to then share pictures of everyone's favorite blue lobster on vacation with you.
- Get tickets to explore Selfie Express for either before or after your aquarium entry time.

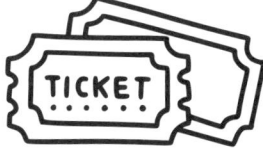

Best Place to Introduce Kids to Live Theater

THE FABULOUS FOX THEATRE

527 N Grand Blvd. | 314-534-1111
fabulousfox.com

You'll be in awe of the majestic atmosphere! Originally opened in 1929 as a movie theater, the Fabulous Fox Theatre transitioned to stage productions in the 1980s and is the perfect place for introducing a younger generation to Broadway! From the breathtaking chandelier to the intricate wood carvings, the unique theater lives up to its name of Fabulous. If your child has difficulty sitting still, select shows will have matinees that are perfect to enjoy, allowing for families to attend a performance without the worry of interrupting others.

✓ How to be a best mom:

- Arrive early so kids can see the historic pipe organ, explore halls of past performance posters, get pictures taken sitting in the throne-like chairs throughout, and grab a snack before the show.
- Take the kids on a Saturday morning tour to experience the theater in a whole new way.

You'll be in awe of the majestic atmosphere!

THE MUNY (MUNICIPAL THEATRE ASSOCIATION OF ST. LOUIS)

1 Theatre Dr. | 314-361-1900
muny.org

You'll develop a love for theater! Forest Park holds a piece of history that is not only the oldest (opened in 1919) and largest (almost 11,000 seats) outdoor theater in the country, but is a goal of many performers who hope to grace its stage. With over 1,450 free seats, the Muny's mission has always been to bring the magic of musical theater to everyone, making it perfect for families to attend together. Don't be surprised if special performances by Muny Kids and Muny Teens inspire your child to try out the stage!

✓ How to be a best mom:

- A picnic dinner on the Muny lawn while listening to preshow entertainment can create a fun memory.
- Plan on visiting concessions for delicious treats, and be sure to enter the Build-A-Bear raffle at the free seats entrance.

STAGES ST. LOUIS

210 E Monroe Ave., Kirkwood | 314-821-2407
stagesstlouis.org

You'll do more than just watch great theater! Right in the heart of Kirkwood is this newer-to-the-area stage, and it's the perfect place to immerse kids in all things theater. The academy has camps (held out in Chesterfield) for kids to learn what it takes to make it on the stage and either be introduced to this artistic niche or better train their theatrical abilities. Classes are available for all ages, and kids are sure to want to audition for a show. Of course there are also amazing productions that you can get tickets for so kids (and the entire family) can enjoy watching great theater without putting on the show themselves.

✓ How to be a best mom:

- Get a treat either before or after a show from Tropical Moose (seasonal) or Clementine's Naughty & Nice Creamery.
- Get season tickets so you never miss a show.

Best Place to Introduce Art

LAUMEIER SCULPTURE PARK

12580 Rott Rd., Sappington | 314-615-5278
laumeiersculpturepark.org

You'll experience an art museum that's outside! There are more than 70 larger-than-life sculptures that are so very unique. Where else can you see a giant eyeball? Think of nature as part of the art, too, with the several walking paths and trails that exist around the property. Some are paved and others more rustic, but there are a variety to choose from to fit different ages and abilities. The Eastern Woodland Trail, with its 1.4-mile loop, is part of the St. Louis County Parks 30/30 Hikes Program since it takes only 30 minutes to complete. There's a whole slew of activities and events throughout the year, including amazing summer camps.

✓ How to be a best mom:

- Start a tradition of attending the annual art fair—art, live music, entertainment, food vendors, and hands-on activities for the entire family!
- Take along sketchbooks and have the kids draw their favorite art structure.

SAINT LOUIS ART MUSEUM

1 Fine Arts Dr. | 314-721-0072
slam.org

You'll marvel at world-renowned art for free! It's uncommon to have access to such beautiful collections without having to pay an entrance fee, making this museum a true gem allowing all to experience fine art. Originally part of the 1904 World's Fair, the massive stone building houses three floors of culture. From watercolor to sketches to classic to modern to Renaissance to everything in between, there's a piece of art to attract the eye of any beholder. There's even ornate antique furniture on display as well as sculptures outside. It's the perfect place to roam on a rainy day or sit down and analyze the lines on canvas.

How to be a best mom:

- Take a break with a bakery treat from the café.
- Attend one of the kid-friendly movies that are part of the Art Hill Film Series during summer.

CONTEMPORARY ART MUSEUM

3750 Washington Blvd. | 314-535-4660
camstl.org

You'll find that St. Louis always wins when it comes to the arts that are free! The building itself speaks contemporary with a glass and concrete boxed-in look from the outside that opens up to a vast space on the inside. Rooms throughout are also clean lines of concrete and solid painted walls as to not detract from the colorful artwork. Even the partial dividing walls are more clean-lined backdrops. This art museum is constantly changing with various exhibits coming and going, so nothing is permanent. On the second floor you will find a quiet place to sit and read that's next to a nook just for kids. The kids will love creating their own art in this small space, building and reading any number of the artsy books geared toward young minds on the shelves.

How to be a best mom:

- Plan on getting a group of kids together and request a private tour of the CAM to take the art experience to the next level.
- Look on the museum's schedule for free events like play date art activities and fun family parties.

Best Place to Introduce Music

NATIONAL BLUES MUSEUM

615 Washington Ave.
314-925-0016
nationalbluesmuseum.org

You'll feel the rhythm and blues! This nonprofit museum is all about sharing the love of the blues and helping to bring music to the community. Seasonally there are free concerts held just outside of the museum on Saturdays. Inside, there are many interactive displays, with a popular one being a soundproof room where you can put on headphones and do a jam session with shaker, spoons, bones, and washboard instruments. Kids will love singing from the old-time-style microphone on the small podium stage and marveling at the case displaying a collection of more than 900 harmonicas. A fun and educational experience, there's even a family membership available to go again and again.

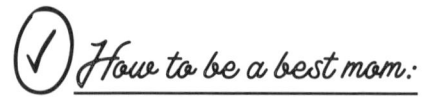

✓ How to be a best mom:

- Buy a harmonica from the gift shop. Your ears might not love it, but your kids sure will.
- Donate and ask that it go toward bringing instruments to underprivileged schools.

POWELL HALL

718 N Grand Blvd. | 314-534-1700
slso.org

You'll relax to the playing of string instruments! Home to the St. Louis Symphony, this venue will immediately have you in awe as you gaze around at the sweeping staircases, plush red carpets, and intricate and stunning chandeliers. Powell Hall has long been known as the place for schoolkids to be introduced to professional music. As a family, you do not have to wait for the field trip because there are family concerts designed specifically for you. There are also free community concerts throughout the area to enjoy, the kickoff to the season concert that's held in Forest Park being the most popular one. It's orchestra music at its finest and a beautiful introduction to elegant ensembles.

✓ How to be a best mom:

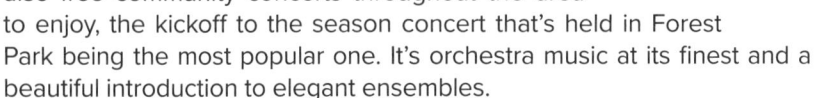

- Christmastime is when SLSO is most decked out, so be sure to attend a holiday concert to see the breathtaking decorations.
- Get tickets to a film concert series (movie on the big screen with music performed by the orchestra) at the Stifel Theatre downtown.

THE FACTORY

17105 N Outer 40 Rd., Chesterfield | 314-423-8500
thefactorystl.com

You'll band together with the music! Located in the District in Chesterfield and set in trendy industrial style, this concert venue is a great place to introduce the kids to your favorite heavy metal band or soft rock sensation. From well-known artists to those with smaller followings and local bands, there's a line of music shows to peruse. While the venue is smaller than a mega concert stadium, it's historically a great place to catch new artists before they make it big. Olivia Rodrigo performed at The Factory in the same month that she won three Grammys in 2022. Kids will love making memories and rocking out with you at their first or 10th concert.

✓ How to be a best mom:

- Take earplugs or sound-blocking earmuffs to protect the hearing.
- Attend a holiday-themed show in December.

Best Splash Pad

CITYGARDEN

801 Market St.
citygardenstl.org/visit

You'll cool off in an oasis right in the middle of downtown! Water features abound in this city favorite. Kids will squeal with delight when running through the 102 pop jets and while watching just how high the water shoots up in the air. In addition to those many vertical water jets, there are also other fountains to enjoy and several pools for kids to splash around in. Ample amounts of beautiful green-space art are found in the two city blocks.

✓ How to be a best mom:

- Take your kids to experience any number of the special musical events held on the plaza during spring and summer.
- Make a day of it by first exploring a different area attraction in the morning before changing into swimwear to visit this unique aquatic spot.

TILLES PARK

9551 Litzsinger Rd.
stlouiscountymo.gov/st-louis-county-departments/parks/places/tilles-park

You'll be deceived by a plaza of concrete! This park has an entire area dedicated to spraying fountains. Over 25 pop jets spray out at random to keep kids guessing as to when the water will make an appearance. Kids will enjoy sitting on a large rock in the center as water sprays all around them. In addition to the popular splash pad there's a massive playground, and it's always a fun time to check out the ducks swimming in the nearby pond.

✓ How to be a best mom:

- Take along a stroller so you can do some loops on the fitness trail.
- Ride through a winter wonderland of lights during the holiday season.

VETERANS TRIBUTE PARK

1031 Kisker Rd., Weldon Spring
sccmo.org/1984/Veterans-Tribute-Park

You'll splash beneath a silo from 1916! It's a bit of a drive for some, but so worth it. This splash pad has everything from a half dozen pop jets to a water trough that comes from above. The jets spray in varying intervals in different directions, and there's even water coming from a rock wall. Perhaps the neatest feature is the wading pool that leads to a concrete floor stream for kids to play in. The man-made stream is a great highlight as well. It's fun for all ages and the perfect place to cool off.

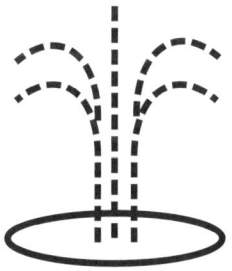

✓ How to be a best mom:

- Take along a cardboard box to fold flat and slide down the artificial turf hill on the playground.
- Don't miss the storybook trail to walk and read pages as you go along the lake.

Best Ropes Course

RYZE ADVENTURE PARK

12420 Grace Church Rd., Maryland Heights | 314-886-7993
ryzeadventure.com

You'll experience a playground adventure like you never have before! Clipping into the safety harness to then roam all over this four-story tower will put courage to the test for ages 8 and up. Filled with obstacles and fun, at times kids will wonder the best way to complete the puzzle. The Adventure Tower also has two zip lines. There's a smaller course for kids ages 4 to 7 to explore on the first level of the tower. Kids will enjoy the view from the observation deck, and those who are really brave will take the plunge from the 40-foot drop all the way to the ground.

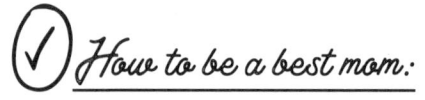

✓ How to be a best mom:

- Try out the mini golf that feels more like a real course than traditional Putt-Putt.
- Look for the free yard games to stay entertained either while waiting to climb or after your adventure.

UNION STATION ROPES COURSE

201 S 18th St. | 314-923-3900
stlouisunionstation.com/rope-course

You'll go to new heights just steps away from an old train yard! There's a course for every member of the family in this three-story exciting attraction. The younger members of the family (less than 48 inches tall) will enjoy feeling like the big kids on their own mini challenge at ground level. Older children will find adventure as they climb high above the concourse that leads to the other attractions at Union Station. The real thrill seekers will make the leap on the zip line to finish out the course or carefully navigate a ledge that is mere inches wide.

✓ How to be a best mom:

- Make sure all participants are wearing shoes with a closed toe and heel.
- Try out any number of the many delicious snacks on-site, particularly the cookies and cupcakes just across the hall.

GO APE

13219 Streetcar Dr., Maryland Heights | 800-971-8271
goape.com/location/missouri-st-louis

You'll climb and swing through the trees in Creve Coeur Lake Memorial Park! This ropes course is completely outdoors and in a serene, wooded setting. Keep an eye out for deer as you make your way through the trees. The suspended bridges and obstacles of this adventure are all under a canopy of trees. There's a training area for learning how to hook in and learning the ropes. In addition to all the climbing, kids will enjoy zipping through the wooded areas on the different zip lines. These lines range in distance from 200 to 500 feet. More than just a ropes course, this adventure park is natural fun with something for all ages to enjoy.

✓ How to be a best mom:

- Bring a pair of work gloves for the adventure, and check in advance online for height and age requirements.
- Book an adventure at night with "Nights at Height."

Best Place for Fall Fun

BROEMMELSIEK PARK

1795 Hwy. DD, Defiance | 636-949-7535
sccmo.org/617/Broemmelsiek-Park

You'll get lost in a free corn maze! A bit outside of the area, but still in St. Charles County, the fall maze at this park covers three acres. Each year there's a different design to set this corn maze apart from the last. The park also hosts a Fall Harvest Festival and old-fashioned hayrides. There's even a special event that can be signed up for called Corn Maze and Caramel Apples that's fun for the entire family. It's held after the corn maze season is over and, in addition to continued maze access, includes a caramel apple station to customize your own fall treat with chocolate, peanuts, M&M's, Oreos, and sprinkles. The event is complete with a campfire to enjoy into the evening.

✓ How to be a best mom:

- Attend the popular Spirits of the Past event at the Historic Daniel Boone Home.
- Start a new family tradition with the Pumpkin Drop at the St. Charles County Regional Airport—Smartt Field.

GREAT GODFREY MAZE

1401 Stamper Ln., Godfrey, IL | 618-466-1483
godfreyil.org/village-township-departments/parks-and-recreation/great-godfrey-corn-maze

You'll love getting lost in fall fun! For over two decades this autumn favorite has become a family tradition for many to make the trek across the Clark Bridge. The destination is part of the local parks department in Godfrey, Illinois, and it's the place to experience a corn maze unlike any other. Each year you will enjoy a different themed corn maze, and there are also fun fall attractions like a cow train made from barrels, hay wagon rides, a corn crib to dig and play among a multitude of kernels, and a large jumping pillow. The younger kids will feel like big kids as they make their way through the mini maze, made from hay bales, not as complex and only one hay bale tall. Older kids will have a scream of a good time after dark when the haunted maze opens.

✓ How to be a best mom:

- Attend the annual fall festival for more fun kids activities like face painting, balloon art, bounce houses, and more.
- Take flashlights when visiting the maze after dark (recommended for kids 10 and older) or purchase a couple at the concession stand.

BROOKDALE FARMS

8004 Twin Rivers Rd., Eureka | 636-938-1005
brookdalefarms.com

You'll watch pumpkins fly high! This farm of fall fun is located just down I-44, and it's the place to see a cannon shoot pumpkins across the sky. There's something for every age group to enjoy. From taking a family hayride to the petting zoo and pony rides, kids will find so much to do here. The 14-acre corn maze is always the biggest draw, and there's a pumpkin patch for finding the perfect jack-o'-lantern. More adventurous older kids and teens who have no fear might want to try out the haunted maze but beware that it's called the Field of Nightmares for a reason. There's no shortage of fun to be had on the playground with a zip line, a ropes course, and swings that resemble hobby horses made from old tires.

✓ How to be a best mom:

- Visit the Sugar Shack for some sweet treats, or stop by the General Store for some holiday-themed items.
- Attend the Balloon Glow held every summer at Brookdale Farms.

Best Toy Store

HAPPY UP INC.

8103 Maryland Ave. | 314-725-2455
happyupinc.com

You'll feel oh so happy! A permanent smile will be on your face as soon as you walk in the door of this fun shop. Staff members are knowledgeable about the toys and pride themselves on having self-tested what's in the shop. This toy store also gives a nod to local game and jewelry makers by having these items featured for sale. Older kids will love the wooden puzzles that become music boxes and constructing DIY miniature kits, while the younger kids will be drawn to the playing-pretend toys like Calico Critters and wooden train sets. Gift wrapping is free, and there's an entire menu book of patterns to choose from. You will not be disappointed by all the finds in store for you in this charming part of Clayton.

How to be a best mom:

- Get an authentic ukulele for your kids to learn at home.
- Visit the Happy Up Inc. store in Edwardsville, Illinois. It's over 3,000 square feet in size!

CIRCLE OF KNOWLEDGE

10980 Sunset Hills Plaza, Sunset Hills | 314-821-5150
circleofknowledge.com

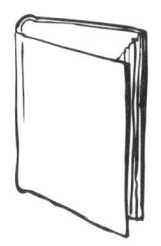

You'll want to build a zip line in your backyard! What started out as a mall toy kiosk over 30 years ago has been in this brick-and-mortar since the early 2000s. This toy store puts the fun in picking out what to play with. The shop itself is bright and colorful with so many different sections designated for the various age groups. Toys have been carefully curated to fit what is on trend with an extensive amount of STEM items. Everything from games, puzzles, ride-ons, books, dolls, trains, and science fun can be found in this one-of-a-kind store. Don't be surprised if one of the popular light-up zip line kits goes home with you.

✓ How to be a best mom:

- Get any number of the educational craft supplies and plan a craft day at your house with friends.
- Purchase a Glennon Card from Cardinal Glennon to give back and save 20 percent at Circle of Knowledge.

CITY SPROUTS

8807 Ladue Rd. | 314-726-9611
citysprouts.com

You'll be reminded of your own childhood the minute you step in the door! While not immediately thought of as your typical toy store, this children's boutique clothing store does have a variety of imaginative and educational play items. From toys for being active outdoors to puzzles and books for quiet time inside, this shop has all the favorites. The whimsical world of Maileg mice can be found here, and children will love collecting the stuffed Danish miniatures. Brands that have been reinstated for a new generation are also represented, and you can find so many unique gifts.

✓ How to be a best mom:

- Find your kids wear from school clothes to festive holiday attire in the back of the store.
- Pick out some books from the Little People, Big Dreams series.

Best Place to Buy Comics and Games

BETTY'S BOOKS

10 Summit Ave., Webster Groves
314-279-1731
bettysbooksstl.com

You'll adventure beyond traditional books! The storefront's awnings and painted reading bench give off a classic bookstore feel, but the novels found within are much more modern. This colorful shop is filled with comics and graphic novels for all ages. There are carefully curated children's books, picture books, and unique gifts as well, all surrounded by vivid murals on the walls. From the graphic novel club to popular Dungeons & Dragons campaigns, kids will enjoy socializing with other comic-loving bookworms. A librarian herself, Betty sure knows her books and has created an environment where all are welcome.

✓ How to be a best mom:

- Purchase a St. Louis Passport to check off places you visit around the city.
- Visit Roger's Produce just around the corner.

GAME NITE

8380 Watson Rd. | 314-270-8440
gameniteshop.com

You'll join other trainers for free open play on Saturdays! One of the most popular social games for kids is Pokemon, so it's no surprise that it's also the favored event held here. This business name might be familiar to you from its presence at the Saint Louis Science Center's First Friday, but there's also an entire game shop to explore. When you walk in you will immediately be immersed in role-playing games available for purchase, complete with buy-in Dungeons & Dragons nights. Both the Dungeon Masters and other participants are more than happy to help kids learn the game. In addition to the rooms of tables and chairs for playing games, there's an entire wall of board games for families to enjoy trying out.

✓ How to be a best mom:

- Purchase a game piece or model for your child to design and create in the painting area.
- Seasonally visit the Christmas tree lot or the snow cone shack housed in the same parking lot.

THE WIZARD'S WAGON

6178 Delmar Blvd. | 314-862-4263
thewizardswagon.square.site

You'll find old-school comics that have been updated for a new generation! This comic book and game shop has nostalgia mixed in with the present day. Sonic the Hedgehog, Scooby-Doo, and My Little Pony have all been resurrected in comic book form for kids to be introduced to. Your kids will also discover all the new trends in trading card games, like Disney Lorcana. Pokemon cards are still a popular draw to the shop, and there are even games for kids to learn how to play. An extensive collection of first-edition comics and graphic novels for all ages round out this enchanting establishment.

✓ How to be a best mom:

- Attend a Lorcana or Dungeons & Dragons event.
- Go miniature golfing just steps away from the shop.

Best Sweet Treats

SUGAR SHACK

151 W Argonne Dr., Kirkwood | 314-966-0065
kirkwoodsugarshack.com

You'll feel a wave of nostalgia with so many sweet treats! For over 15 years this community favorite has been in the heart of downtown Kirkwood. The candy store boasts fun, eclectic decor and a charming wood floor, and it is well known for having over a dozen flavors of cotton candy made in-house. While the colorful candies filling glass canisters in the front window are just for show, there's an array of penny candies for sale from the large candy case. The fun does not stop with nostalgic candy; a line of popular freeze-dried candy is also available. Everything is purposefully priced in 25-cent increments so kids can easily practice math.

✓ *How to be a best mom:*

- Purchase some wooden coins, sweetly called "candy currency," in advance for kids to shop with their own money.

- Plan to start a birthday party at the Sugar Shack by scheduling guests to shop for treats before store hours and then continue the festivities at home.

CROWN CANDY KITCHEN

1401 St. Louis Ave. | 314-621-9650
crowncandykitchen.net

You'll step back in time with an old-fashioned soda fountain and candy shop in one! The favorite destination for generations of locals and visitors first opened in 1913. Classic ice cream flavors and other sweet treats are just the start of a menu that also includes meals. Kids will get a kick out of sitting in the antique booths and taking pictures with the stl250 Cakeway to the West birthday cake out front. An assortment of delicious candies fills the case, and this popular attraction is the place to get chocolate bars with unique phrases and logos.

✓ *How to be a best mom:*

- Order the famous chocolate rabbits for Easter baskets.
- Try to impress your kids by completing the 5 Malt Challenge. The keyword being "try."

UNION STATION SODA FOUNTAIN

201 S 18th St. | 314-923-3939
sodafountain-stl.com

You'll be on sugar overload the minute you walk in the door! Set up like an old-fashioned soda fountain and candy store, this sweet destination has delight written all over it. The colorful atmosphere is so much fun, and you can practically smell the sugar in the air. Jars and barrels of sweets can be found with both new and old favorites. Candy by the pound fills containers up and down the walls, only adding to the vibrant decor. No matter what you choose, your sweet tooth will be satisfied.

✓ *How to be a best mom:*

- Split a Freak Shake—that is a milkshake with lots of candy.
- Balance out the sugar overload with a burger and fries on the soda fountain side.

Best Arcade

ST. LOUIS PINBALL

1517 S 8th St. | stlouispinball.com

You'll delight at all the fun clack and ding sound effects! The glow of the florescent black-lit carpet only adds to the art of pinball in this downtown arcade. Kids will be surprised to find all the flashing lights, catchy tunes, and silver balls being launched inside game boxes in the upstairs of an old brick warehouse. All are part of the experience when it comes to pinballing. You won't find a larger collection of classic and modern pinball machines anywhere else in the area. Every few months there are some new pinball machines brought in to keep things energized.

✓ How to be a best mom:

- Play a round of mini golf on the interactive black-light 1980s-themed course, or have a seat in the lobby area to play a board game.
- Try out an escape room as a family in the same complex.

MAIN EVENT

17027 N Outer 40 Rd., Chesterfield | 636-536-9999
mainevent.com/locations/missouri/chesterfield

You'll find just about every arcade game imaginable! While there's no pinball, this arcade has everything else to make it a gamers' paradise. The adults will feel nostalgic for their own childhood with Monopoly and Plinko-themed games, and there are more than five different types of basketball hoop action. There are so many different classic carnival games in arcade form. An extensive selection of racing games await, from bullet bikes and Mario Kart to monster trucks. Kids can even try out working the slopes on a simulation snowboarding game. Even if the kids don't win something from the giant claw machines, they will love redeeming their tickets in the prize store. Yes, it's really a store that they can shop in using tickets and will be the highlight at the end of an already great time.

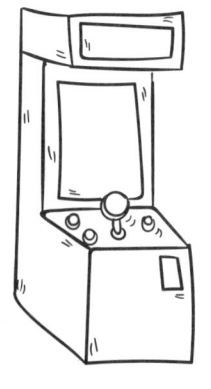

✓ How to be a best mom:

- Take your bikes to the River's Edge Park trail that runs directly behind the Main Event complex.
- Stop off and play some yard games in the District just down the sidewalk that runs out front.

EDISON'S ENTERTAINMENT COMPLEX

2477 S State Rte. 157, Ste. A, Edwardsville, IL | 618-307-9020
edisonsfun.com

You'll find a game for every age! It's about a 20-minute drive to this destination on the Illinois side of the river but worth checking out since the complex has so much to do in one place. There's an assortment of arcade game sections for different ages to enjoy. Jr. Inventors Zone has arcade games the toddler crowd can play, and there's even an entire room called the High Ticket Zone that's dedicated to bigger ticket payouts. Reloadable gaming cards are tap-to-play with no swiping involved, making it easier for kids to get the game started. Parents will love introducing their kids to the classic Pac-Man arcade game, and there are a few virtual reality gaming options for the next generation. Two-player games can also be found in this arcade, and families can have a blast competing with each other at Skee-Ball.

✓ How to be a best mom:

- Play some laser tag in Pharaoh's Quest or reserve some bowling lanes.
- Go for some frozen custard at Bobby's just nine minutes down the road in nearby Maryville, Illinois.

Best Place to Go Sledding

Courtesy of Amanda E. Doyle

ART HILL

1 Fine Arts Dr.

You'll sled down a hill with history! This popular sledding destination has been enjoyed by generations since the year after the 1904 World's Fair. It's said that workers from the fair used folding chairs to sled down the hill in January of 1905 and from there the tradition began. The steep hill descends from the art museum grounds just beyond the majestic *Apotheosis of St. Louis* statue and stops at the edge of the Grand Basin waterway. Gone are the days of using cinders to slow sledders down from entering the water, but the older generation still likes to share the tale. These days there are hay bales set up to prevent such accidents.

✓ How to be a best mom:

- Visit the west lawn of the art museum to find the *Placebo* silver tree to see its shine while reflecting the snow.
- In warmer months, enjoy a movie or attend a concert on Art Hill.

HIDDEN VALLEY SKI RESORT

17409 Hidden Valley Dr., Eureka | 636-938-5373
hiddenvalleyski.com

You'll fly down a mountain of snow without going to the Rockies! With more than 10 lanes dedicated to snow tubing, Polar Plunge is the largest of its kind in Missouri. It's primarily a ski resort, but the smooth-ride tubing lanes have quickly gained in popularity. The tubes are bright in color and comfortable, and they have several handles around the perimeter and a round seat opening to let riders burrow down into the middle. There's a blazing outdoor firepit if you need to warm up, and all will appreciate the conveyor lifts that take both you and your tube back up to the top of the run. Dress warm and have a fun time together on the slopes here, even if you don't ski.

✓ How to be a best mom:

- Get a treat or a delicious hot chocolate at the outdoor Tubing Café.
- Look into lessons or get a lift ticket if your kids would like to try out snow skiing.

COMMUNITY PARK NEAR YOU

You'll ride the slopes practically in your own backyard! Not everyone has a great sledding hill on their property, but there are tons of great hills at various community parks around the area. Deer Creek Park (called Rocketship Park by the locals) in Webster Groves has a super steep hill for the real thrill seekers, as does Crestwood Park. Whitecliff Park has a couple of hills to enjoy, one being more daring and another that is long and slower going. Whether you choose to try a run in Jefferson Barracks or Lindenwood Park, just look for the crowds with sleds after a fresh snow to find the best ones near you.

✓ How to be a best mom:

- Take along a thermos of hot chocolate to warm up those tummies.
- Have the kids race side by side down the slope at the same time.

Best Nursery for Family Gardening

SHERWOOD'S FOREST NURSERY

2651 Barrett Station Rd., Manchester | 314-966-0028
sherwoods-forest.com

You'll begin a family tradition with a true gardening heirloom! For generations families have enjoyed planting trees, shrubs, flowers, and all things green from this delightful nursery. With 10 greenhouses on nine acres of land, this is one of the leading nurseries in the area. Many of the shopping malls in St. Louis have trusted Sherwood's Forest to install their atriums, and a job well done means it's perfect for your own home. This legendary botanical fixture will be sure to grow in your heart as it has for many over the years.

✓ How to be a best mom:

- Attend one of the St. Louis County Parks Children's Garden Club events that Sherwood's Forest has been part of sponsoring for over 25 years.
- Plant a tree (popular ones are the large October glory maple and evergreens) that will grow right along with your family.

ROLLING RIDGE NURSERY

60 N Gore Ave., Webster Groves | 314-962-3311
rollingridgenursery.com

You'll enter a garden oasis in downtown Webster Groves! From vegetable plants to berry bushes to flowering greenery and everything in between, this community favorite has all you need for gardening with your kids. In the expansive garden shop, you'll find a large variety of pet-friendly plants along with ones that are rare and unusual. There are even air plants that are perfect for those lacking a green thumb. Lots of gift ideas can be found in the shop as well, and kids will want to pop in just to have a look around the greenhouse or see if they can spot butterflies floating among the plants in the courtyard.

✓ How to be a best mom:

- Let your child pick out a small pot and plant to take care of in their room at home.
- Try growing a unique honeyberry shrub that yields berries with a sweet and tart flavor.

SUGAR CREEK GARDENS

1011 N Woodlawn Ave., Kirkwood | 314-965-3070
sugarcreekgardens.com

You'll find gardening essentials sitting on soil that is rich in history! The property has been used for gardening for over 100 years. It's even where cut flowers for the 1904 World's Fair were grown. Now a women-owned family business, this gardening center is right in the heart of a community with residential homes as neighbors. There's one greenhouse on-site with everything from vegetable plants to native plants. Kids will enjoy exploring the various types of herbs, fruit trees, and shrubs to help decide what to plant. The most popular plant is butterfly milkweed, an important food source for caterpillars that will one day become monarch butterflies. Kids will find this garden educational as well as beautiful.

✓ How to be a best mom:

- Build a fairy garden in your backyard with items from this gardening center.
- After getting some new plants, drop by Oberweis (less than a quarter of a mile away) for some ice cream.

Best Activity with the Family Dog

SOULARD PET PARADE

stlmardigras.org/events/purina-pet-parade

You'll love getting your pet dressed up for a parade! The largest costumed pet parade in the world isn't just for the dogs, it's fun for the entire family. Held as part of the Soulard Mardi Gras festivities, the pet parade is a family-friendly event that kids are sure to love. Besides on Halloween, when else will you see a four-legged superhero or a dog dressed up as a hot dog? Kids will have a great time getting the furry member of the family ready by planning out the costume and then dressing up. Aim high with the costume, and if you are lucky, your pet might be chosen to be part of parade royalty. These best-dressed pets will then be invited to the coronation party. The parade is free to watch, and families without dogs will still enjoy the festivities as they ooh and ah over all the well-thought-out costumes.

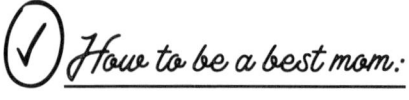

Courtesy of Sarah Johnson

✓ How to be a best mom:

- Take your kids to the Wiener Dog Derby, held in the afternoon, to cheer on racing dachshunds.
- Help your kids make a shoebox float for the parade.

TAILS AND TRAILS DOG PARK

1675 Mason Rd. | 314-615-8472
stlouiscountymo.gov/st-louis-county-departments/parks/places/tails-trails-dog-park

You'll have a great day out with your dog! This five-acre dog park, inside popular Queeny Park, is primarily entry by membership only, but there are day passes available. The double-gated entry offers a secure space for dogs to explore outdoors. Kids will love watching the family dog building skills while running leash free and navigating and jumping over the agility stations. These skill stations aren't just about training pups; they're also an important part of getting exercise. There are even separate areas for big and small dogs.

✓ How to be a best mom:

- After playing at the dog park, leash up and take a stroll on one of the many trails throughout Queeny Park or visit the playground.
- Pet memorial bricks are available in honor of your furry family member.

BARK IN THE PARK

2824 Tower Grove Ave. | 314-951-1565
p2p.onecause.com/barkinthepark2023

You'll 5K with your four-legged friend! Held at Tower Grove Park, this event is a great way to give back to the community by helping to support the Humane Society. In addition to the 5K and one-mile run/walk, there are vendor booths, Purina's Incredible Dog Challenge, and other fun events and activities to choose from right on-site. All proceeds from the registration go to the Humane Society of Missouri's Animal Cruelty Task Force. Kids 12 and under are free and will enjoy the energetic, overall feel of this family festival. Pet contests, silent auctions, food trucks, and so much more are all part of this fantastic occasion. More than just a race or walk in the park, it's a life-changing event.

✓ How to be a best mom:

- Get your kids involved with fundraising before the event.
- Test out your furry family member's skill on the doggy agility course.

fun IDEA

Best Movie Theater

B&B THEATRES

12657 Olive Blvd., Creve Coeur
314-789-3130
bbtheatres.com/our-theatres/
g01i1-b-and-b-creve-coeur-west-olive-
10-wb-roll-bowling

You'll say "this is so cool" over and over again everywhere you turn! This unique movie theater definitely puts the wow factor back in the movies. From the bowling alley with bowling balls that look like giant pool balls to the fantastic arcade to delicious eats, families will enjoy so much more than just a regular movie-viewing experience. Truly an action-park-level cinema, there's even a special Screen Play theater that allows kids to get their wiggles out (before the movie starts) in the massive play area taking up the entire side of the auditorium's wall. This dedicated-to-families theater room also has slightly lower sound playing through the speakers. Don't worry, there are other theater rooms without the play area feature.

✓ How to be a best mom:

- Reserve a bowling lane ahead of time.
- Request to have your arcade cards combined so kids can share the bigger prize.

MARCUS RONNIE'S CINEMA

5320 S Lindbergh Blvd. | 314-756-9325
marcustheatres.com

You'll experience a part of St. Louis history while watching a movie! What began in the late 1940s as a drive-in, this favorite movie theater has indeed morphed from varying screen sizes to multiplex over the years. The full-service theater has everything from 20 screens to a large arcade to all the best snack and delicious meal options to enjoy while watching a movie. Guests will even catch a glimpse into the past with a nod to Ronnie's early days when enjoying a meal and watching a sporting event on the big screen in the lobby from a car-shaped booth. The popular family film series has specials on food and previously released movies all summer long, the perfect way to beat the heat for a few hours indoors.

✓ How to be a best mom:

- Rent out an auditorium for a fun and unique birthday party.
- Join the loyalty program to earn points on purchases.

SKYVIEW DRIVE-IN

5700 N Belt W, Belleville, IL | 618-233-4400
skyview-drive-in.com

You'll watch a movie under the stars! This drive-in has been in business since 1949 and it's the only one within 75 miles. There are two screens: #1 is 105 feet wide with spots for 420 cars, and #2 is 75 feet wide with spots for 185 cars. Gone are the days of vintage speakers on the pole, but you can tune into the movie's sound on your car radio. Each night has a double feature of newly released movies, and kids will enjoy playing on the playground in front of the screen before the movie starts. There's a concession stand that serves cheeseburgers, hot dogs, french fries, nachos, pickles, popcorn, soda, and candy. It's sure to become a family tradition for years to come during the summer months.

✓ How to be a best mom:

- For an additional fee, reserve a spot to watch from your favorite view.
- Take lawn chairs and a battery-operated radio to enjoy the movie while sitting outside in front of your vehicle.

Index

9 Mile Garden, 68
Aerie's Alpine Coaster, 107
Aloha Mini Golf, 79
Alton, Illinois, 49, 53
Amp Up, 110
Apple Butter Festival, 119
Aquaport, 105
Arcades, 78, 83, 110–111, 140–141, 148–149
Art Hill, 29, 125, 142
Art museum, 44, 124–125, 142
Axe throwing, 110
B&B Theatres, 148
Babler State Park, 31
Balloon animals, 115
Ballpark Village, 4, 67, 115
Bark in the Park, 147
Barn, The, 75
Batting cages, 80
Bee Tree Park, 43
Betty's Books, 136
Big Age Gaps, 16
Bike Stop Café, 57
Birthday party, 21, 58, 76–77, 83, 94–95, 99, 101, 110–111, 112–113, 138, 149
Blissfully Popped Popcorn, 59
Bluff View Park, 95
Board games, 66, 91, 137, 140
Boathouse at Forest Park, 29, 70
Bobby's Frozen Custard, 141
Bocce ball, 80
Book clubs, 58–59, 60
Book House, The, 59
Bowlero, 83
Bowling, 82–83, 141, 148
Brentwood Park, 9
Broemmelsiek Park, 132
Brookdale Farms, 133
Brunch with Santa, 115
Buder Park, 97
Build-A-Bear Adventure, 111
Bumper boats, 111
Bumper cars, 100, 111
Busch Stadium, 4
Butterfly House, 20, 87, 121
Cahokia Mounds, 34–35
Candy Cane Lane, 3, 63
Car shows, 93

Cardinals Nation, 67, 115
Carousel, 7, 16, 19, 87, 109, 117
Carrollton Park, 15
Cathedral Basilica of St. Louis, The, 3, 7
Checkered Flag Hobby Country, 93
Chess, 14, 48, 91
Children's Garden, 121, 144
Chocolate Chocolate Chocolate Company, 109
Christmas trees, 5, 53, 63, 115, 137
Circle of Knowledge, 135
Circus Flora, 17
City Foundry STL, 69
City Museum, 6
City Sprouts, 135
Citygarden, 128
Clementine's Naughty & Nice Creamery, 63, 81, 123
Climatron, 5, 121
Climbing, 6, 8–9, 11, 15, 21, 25, 33, 38, 102, 116, 120, 131
Clydesdales, 18, 36
Columbia Bottom Conservation Area, 89
Comics, 107, 136–137
Contemporary Art Museum St. Louis, 125
Corn mazes, 53, 132–133
Corner Pub & Grill, The, 74
Covered bridges, 41, 87
Cowboy Critters, 113
Crafting, 10–11, 12, 76, 135
Crestwood Bowl, 82
Crestwood, Missouri, 73, 75, 82
Crestwood Park, 143
Creve Coeur, Missouri, 29, 53, 148
Creve Coeur Airport, 97
Creve Coeur Lake, 15, 29, 131
Crown Candy Kitchen, 139
Cuivre River State Park, 31
Cunetto House of Pasta, 71
Dad's Cookie Company, 3
Dandy Soft Serve, 113
Daniel Boone Library Branch, 61
Deer Creek Park, 143
Defiance, Missouri, 37, 41, 132
Delmar Loop, 64, 73, 78
Dinosaurs, 17, 42, 98

Disc golf, 15, 23, 91
Discovery Zone, 61
Disney Lorcana, 137
Dogs, 13, 25, 48, 57, 63, 146–147
Downtown St. Louis, 2–3, 5, 27, 35, 45, 73, 84, 90, 99, 127, 128, 140
Dungeons & Dragons, 136–137
Eads Bridge, 5
Eagles, 39, 91, 101
Eckert's, 52
Edwardsville, Illinois, 37, 134, 141
Edward "Ted" and Pat Jones- Confluence Point State Park, 49
Elephant Rocks State Park, 33
Ellisville, Missouri, 61
Emerson Grand Basin, 29
Emmenegger Nature Park, 47
Endangered Wolf Center, 41
Escape room, 140
Eureka, Missouri, 25, 41, 107, 133, 143
Fabulous Fox Theatre, The, 67, 122
Face painting, 111, 112, 115, 133
Factory, The, 127
Fall fun, 51, 132–133
Family Golf and Learning Center, 81
Faust Park, 19, 87
Federhofer's Bakery, 65
Ferris wheels, 6, 78
Festival of Nations, 119
Festival of the Little Hills, 57
Festivals, 33, 43, 88, 100, 118–119, 132–133, 147
Figure skating, 101
Fishing, 9, 42–43, 31, 38–39
Fitz's, 64, 113
FlowRider, 105
Forest Park, 3, 5, 7, 17, 19, 29, 34, 42, 44, 46, 56, 70, 81, 100, 113, 118, 123, 127
Foristel, Missouri, 9
Fountain on Locust, The, 65
Fredbird, 115
Free admission, 121
Frisco Train & Toy Store, 95
Frontenac, Missouri, 114
Frontier Park, 57
Frozen custard, 63, 81, 92, 141
Game Nite, 137
Games, 39, 66–67, 68, 84, 91, 118, 130, 135, 136–137, 141
Garden Glow, 116
Gardening, 144–145

Gateway Arch, 2–3, 27
Gateway Grizzlies, 84
Geocaching, 46–47
Giving Back, 45
Glassblowing, 5
Glen Carbon, Illinois, 37
Glenco, Missouri, 24, 95
Go Ape, 131
Godfrey, Illinois, 133
Golf lesson, 81
Golfing, 80–81
Gondolas, 16, 107
Grafton, Illinois, 91, 101, 107
Grand Center District, 17
Grand Hall, 90, 115
Grandma's Playroom, 11
Grant's Farm, 36, 109, 117
Grant's Trail, 18, 22, 36, 75, 103
Graphic novels, 136–137
Gray Summit, Missouri, 13, 86
Great Forest Park Balloon Race, The, 118
Great Godfrey Maze, 133
Great Rivers Greenway, 9, 47
Happy Up Inc., 134
Hayrides, 39, 132–133
HealthWorks, 99
Helicopter tours, 5
Hi-Pointe Drive-In, 72
Hidden Valley Ski Resort, 143
High school sports, 85, 101
Highlands Golf & Tennis, The, 81
Hiking, 21, 25, 33, 38–39, 91
Hill, The, 71
Hillsboro, Missouri, 87
Historic Aircraft Restoration Museum, 97
Historic Daniel Boone Home, 41, 132
History, 2, 4, 7, 17, 19, 32, 34–35, 37–38, 49, 53, 57, 75, 97, 109, 123, 145, 149
Hobby shop, 92
Hockey, 80, 85, 101
Holiday lights, 3, 116–117
Holiday Lights at Grant's Farm, 117
Holidays, 13, 87, 115
Horseback riding, 91
Hot-air balloons, 118
Huzzah River, 27
Huzzah Valley Resort, 27
I Love Forest Park 5K and Kids Fun Run, 44

151

Ice cream, 4, 59, 62–63, 64–65, 69, 71, 75, 81, 113, 123, 139, 145
Ice-skating, 9, 100–101
Ices Plain & Fancy, 62
Imo's Pizza, 71
Imperial, Missouri, 40
Indian Camp Creek Park, 9
Indoor play area, 10
James S. McDonnell Planetarium, 17, 42, 98
Jefferson Barracks, 15, 35, 143
Jefferson Lake, 42
Jewel Box, 19, 56
Jones-Confluence Point State Park, 49
Junior Ranger Program, 2–3, 18
JustServe, 55
Katy Trail, 37
Kids Empire, 21
Kilwins, 59
Kimmswick, Missouri, 119
Kinetic Park, 102
Kirkwood, Missouri, 21, 36, 47, 51, 60, 63, 72–73, 81, 93, 120, 123, 138, 145
Kirkwood Farmers' Market, 51
Kirkwood Park, 47
Kirkwood Public Library, 60
Kitchen Conservatory, 77
Klondike Park, 30
Landing, The, 69
Landing Hub, The, 91
Laser tag, 110, 141
Laumeier Sculpture Park, 124
Laura's Run 4 Kids, 45
Lewis and Clark, 48–49, 57
Lewis & Clark Boat House and Museum, 48
Libraries, 18, 32, 43, 49, 55, 59, 60–61, 97
Light shows, 13, 17, 90
Lincoln, Abraham, 32
Lindenwood Park, 143
Little Free Library, 18, 43, 55
Loading Dock Ice Rink, The, 101
Lodge Des Peres, The, 105
Logan University, 15
Lone Elk Park, 38–39
Mad Science, 99
Madison County Transit, 37
Magic House, The, 120

Magic House MADE for Kids, The, 12, 120
Magic Mini Golf, 78
Magic shows, 112
Main Event, 141
Main Street Books, 59
Major Lee Berra Creation Station, 11
Manchester, Missouri, 144
Maplewood, Missouri, 59
Marais Temps Clair Conservation Area, 96
Marcus Ronnie's Cinema, 149
Mardi Gras, 146
Margaret Atalanta Park, 57
Market Street, 90, 128
Maryland Heights, Missouri, 15, 23, 29, 97, 105, 130–131
Mastodon State Historic Site, 40
Mathilda-Welmering Park, 65
Maypop Coffee & Garden Shop, 57
Memberships, 6, 19, 81, 94, 98–99, 120–121, 126, 147
Meramec Caverns, 26
Meramec Greenway, 24, 93
Meramec River, 24, 26, 81, 93, 97
Meramec Trail, 97
Mini Golf, 16, 69, 78–79, 111, 130, 140
Mississippi River, 2–3, 27, 33, 34–35, 43, 49, 88, 91, 107
Missouri Botanical Garden, 5, 86, 116, 121
Missouri History Museum, 34
Missouri River, 37, 48–49, 57, 96
Moline Acres, Missouri, 49
Muckerman Fountain, 119
Muny, 44, 70, 123
Myron and Sonya Glassberg Family Conservation Area, 25
Myseum, 13
National Blues Museum, 126
National Museum of Transportation, The, 11, 94
Nature Playscape, 19, 46
North Central Hobbies, 92
Novel Neighbor, The, 58
Nutcracker on Ice, 101
O'Fallon, Missouri, 76
Old Courthouse, 3
Old Spaghetti Factory, The, 69
Olivette, Missouri, 83
Olivette Lanes, 83
Our Lady of the Rivers Shrine, 96

152

Our Lady of the Snows, 3
Overland, Missouri, 92
Pacific, Missouri, 91
Paint Louis, 88
Pancakes, 75, 115
Pancakes with Santa, 115
Pappy's Smokehouse, 73
Parks, 31, 33, 35, 36, 124, 133, 143, 144
Pasta, 51, 69, 71, 77
Patty's Cheesecake. 79
Pere Marquette Lodge, 91
Petting zoos, 20, 113, 119, 133
Picnic Island, 29
Pieces Board Game Bar & Cafe, 66
Pizza, 69, 71, 77, 110
Play Street Museum, 10
Playgrounds, 8–9, 19, 21, 22–23, 24–25, 28, 31, 33, 36–37, 39, 40, 43, 50, 55, 57, 80, 84, 87, 89, 93, 95, 103, 104–105, 106, 129, 130, 133, 147, 149
Plaza Frontenac, 114
Pokemon, 137
Polar Express Train Ride, The, 115
Popeye, 33
Portage Des Sioux, Missouri, 96
Powder Valley Conservation Nature Center, 21
Powell Hall, 127
Premier Entertainment, 112
Pumpkin patches, 51, 133
Purina Farms, 13
Puttshack, 69, 79
Queeny Park, 25, 147
Ramp Riders, 103
Rayburn Park, 22
Riverfront, 2, 5
Rivers, 2–3, 24, 26–27, 31, 33, 34–35, 37, 43, 48–49, 52, 57, 81, 88, 91, 93, 97, 101, 107, 121, 141
Rolling Ridge Nursery, 145
Root beer, 29, 64, 113
Ropes courses, 110, 130–131, 133
Ryze Adventure Park, 130
Saint Louis Art Museum, 44, 125, 142
Saint Louis Billikens, 85
Saint Louis Science Center, 17, 98, 137
Saint Louis Zoo, 7, 44, 80
Salt + Smoke, 73

Sandy Creek Covered Bridge State Historic Site, 87
Santa, 53, 114–115, 117
Sappington House Barn Restaurant, 36, 75
Sappington House Museum, 75
Sauget, Illinois, 84
Schnucks Cooking School, 77
Science, 13, 17, 98–99, 113, 135, 137
Selfie Express, 121
Selfie WRLD, 89
Sensory gardens, 8 19, 86
Shack, The, 74
Shaved ice, 47, 51, 79
Shaw Nature Reserve, 86, 121
Shaw neighborhood, 62
Shaw Park, 8
Sherwood's Forest Nursery, 144
Simpson Lake, 28
Six Flags, 91, 107
Skeeters Frozen Custard, 92
Skyview Drive-In, 149
Slick City Action Park, 106
Slides, 6, 8–9, 10, 13, 19, 21, 61, 99, 105, 106, 120
Slot cars, 92
Smartt Field Airport (St. Charles County Regional Airport), 96, 132
Snacks, 4, 8, 17, 37, 47, 50, 61, 69, 98, 107, 122, 131, 149
Snow skiing, 143
Soda fountain, 65, 67, 139
Soulard Farmers Market, 51, 66
Soulard Pet Parade, 146
South County, Missouri, 15, 64, 93
Splash pads, 8–9, 23, 35, 50, 128–129
Sports, 63, 71, 84–85, 102
Springfield, Illinois, 32
Stage Left Grille, 67
STAGES St. Louis, 123
Staycations, 90–91
Steinberg Skating Rink, 100
Stifel Theatre, 127
St. Louis Aquarium at Union Station, 121
St. Louis Car Museum & Sales, 93
St. Louis Cardinals, 3, 4, 80, 115
St. Louis Carousel, 19, 87
St. Louis County Library, 49, 61
St. Louis Graffiti Wall, 88
St. Louis Orienteering Club, 47

St. Louis Pinball, 140
St. Louis Symphony, 127
St. Louis Union Station Hotel, 90
St. Louis Union Station Soda Fountain, 139
St. Louis Wheel, 16
Strawberry Festival, 119
Story time, 11, 34
Sugar Creek Gardens, 145
Sugar Shack, 133, 138
Sugarfire Smoke House, 70, 72
Sullivan, Missouri, 26
Summer camp, 58, 77, 81, 99, 121, 124
Summer reading program, 60–61
Sunflowers, 53, 89
Sunset Hills, Missouri, 135
Sweetology, 76
Swimming lessons, 105
Swimming pools, 90–91, 104–105, 128–129
Swing-A-Round Fun Town, 111
Tails and Trails Dog Park, 25, 147
Tangled Tinsel Christmas Tree Farm, 53
Ted Drewes, 63
Teenagers, 14–15, 17, 59, 82, 85, 123, 133
Tennis, 81, 85
Theater, 99, 122–123
Thies Farm and Market, 53
Tilles Park, 117, 129
Toddlers, 6, 10–11, 21, 121, 141
Tours, 2–3, 4–5, 6–7, 18, 26, 32, 41, 75, 93, 107, 108–109, 119, 121, 122, 125
Tower Grove Farmers' Market, 50
Tower Grove Park, 50, 119, 147
Tower Grove, Missouri, 119
Tower Tee, 80
Town and Country, Missouri, 13, 110
Toy stores, 95, 134–135

Toys, 30, 93, 134–135
Trading cards, 118, 137
Train rides, 7, 11, 94–95, 115
Trains, 11, 95, 135
Trams, 109, 121
Troy, Missouri, 31
Turkey Trot, 45
Ulysses S. Grant National Historic Site, 18, 36
Uncle Bill's, 75
Union Station, 16, 90, 115, 121, 131, 139
Upper Limits Rock Gym & Pro Shop, 15
Vago Park, 23
Valley Park, Missouri, 28, 38–39, 79, 83, 95, 97
Vat19, 108
Veterans Tribute Park, 129
Virtual reality, 110, 141
Vlasis Park, 43
Volunteer, 35, 54–55, 103
Wabash Frisco & Pacific Railroad, 95
Wapelhorst Aquatic Facility, 104
Water parks, 104, 107
Waterslides, 104–105
Watson Trail Park, 23
Webster Groves, Missouri, 57–58, 101, 136, 143, 145
Webster Groves Ice Arena, 101
Weldon Spring, Missouri, 37, 129
West Alton, Missouri, 49
Whitecliff Park, 143
Wildwood, Missouri, 24, 31, 95
Winter wonderlands, 116–117, 129
Wizard's Wagon, The, 137
Wooden trains, 95, 134
World Bird Sanctuary, 39
World's Fair Pavilion, 19, 44, 70
Yoga, 11
Youth Aviation Day, 97
Zip lines, 9, 22–23, 130–131, 133, 135